HEBREW LETTERS & NUMBERS

ALEPH TO CHET

VOLUME 1

RABBI JASON SOBEL

FUSION
WITH RABBI JASON
TM

Hebrew Letters & Numbers Companion Guide, Volume 1

Copyright © 2025 by Rabbi Jason Sobel

Printed by Amazon.

RJS Publishing
5062 Lankershim Blvd., Suite 3017
North Hollywood, CA 91601

www.fusionglobal.org

For information about purchasing this title in bulk please email info@fusionglobal.org.

Cover photograph of Hebrew scroll copyright © by Mission Media on Lightstock.

Cover photograph of an open Bible copyright © by Prixel Creative on Lightstock.

Design and typesetting by Jorie Lee.

Unless otherwise noted all Scripture in this book is taken from the Holy Scriptures, Tree of Life Version. Copyright © 2014, 2016 by the Tree of Life Bible Society. Used by permission of the Tree of Life Bible Society.

Scripture quotations marked NIV are taken from the Holy Bible, New International Version® Copyright 1973, 1978, 1984, 2011 by Biblica Inc.™ Used by permission of Zondervan. All rights reserved worldwide. www.zondervan.com. The "NIV" and "New International Version" are trademarks registered in the United States Patent and Trademark Office by Biblica, Inc.™

Scripture quotations marked NASB are taken from the New American Standard Bible®, Copyright © 1960, 1962, 1963, 1968, 1971, 1972, 1973, 1975, 1977, 1995, by The Lockman Foundation. Used by permission.

Scripture quotations marked KJV are taken from the King James Version of the Bible.

Scripture quotations marked NKJV are from the New King James Version®, © 1982 by Thomas Nelson. Used by permission. All rights reserved.

Scripture quotations marked ESV are from The ESV Bible® (The Holy Bible, English Standard Version®), copyright © 2001 by Crossway, a publishing ministry of Good News Publishers. Used by permission. All rights reserved.

Scripture quotations marked NLT are taken from the *Holy Bible*, New Living Translation, copyright © 1996, 2004, 2015 by Tyndale House Foundation. Used by permission of Tyndale House Publishers, Inc., Carol Stream, Illinois 60188. All rights reserved.

Note: Throughout the book the author has emphasized certain words within the Bible text with boldface.

Contents

Hebrew Alphanumeric Chart

Letter	Name	Value	Letter	Name	Value
א	Aleph	1	ל	Lamed	30
ב	Bet	2	מ ם	Mem	40
ג	Gimel	3	נ ן	Nun	50
ד	Dalet	4	ס	Samekh	60
ה	Hei	5	ע	Ayin	70
ו	Vav	6	פ ף	Peh	80
ז	Zayin	7	צ ץ	Tsadee	90
ח	Cheit	8	ק	Qof	100
ט	Tet	9	ר	Resh	200
י	Yod	10	ש	Shin	300
כ ך	Kaf	20	ת	Tav	400

Overview

I'm Rabbi Jason Sobel, and I'd like to welcome you to Hebrew letters and numbers. I am looking forward to going on this journey with you. There is so much incredible wisdom and revelation in the Hebrew numbers and letters. God loves numbers. The Bible is full of numbers, words, and letters that give us a deeper meaning into what God wants us to know about Him and His message to us.

Let me begin by briefly sharing a few foundational thoughts you will need to understand as we start this journey.

First, there's tremendous significance in every Hebrew letter. Hebrew letters are the building blocks of Creation from a spiritual perspective because God spoke the world into existence with words, and words contain letters. We can think of the letters as the spiritual DNA of all of Creation. The shape and arrangement of the Hebrew letters are important, but Hebrew letters are also alphanumeric, and that characteristic is essential for everything that we do in our study. Not many alphabets are alphanumeric, but Hebrew is. This means individual letters also symbolize numbers. In other words, every letter has a numerical value, and the way numbers are written in Hebrew is with letters. For example, suppose I'm preaching or speaking in Hebrew, and I ask you, "I want you to open your Bible to Genesis Chapter 1, verse 1." I'd say, "Open your

BERESHEET

בְּרֵאשִׁית

Bibles to *Beresheet* (that's the Hebrew name of Genesis), *Aleph*, *Aleph* (Chapter 1, verse 1). *Aleph* is the first letter of the Hebrew alphabet; it has a numerical value of one. When you open the Hebrew Bible to Chapter 1, you'll see a letter *Aleph* representing Chapter 1 and a smaller *Aleph* representing verse 1. Chapter 2, verse 1, would be *Bet Aleph* (Chapter 2, verse 1 as *Bet* is the second letter in the Hebrew alphabet). Each letter of the Hebrew alphabet represents a numeric value.

God's Creation Code

Letters are the building blocks of Creation. From a scientific perspective, this often doesn't make sense. We live in a mathematical universe. God's speaking the world into existence, in the world of scientific thought, is a myth. The scientific community typically rejects any claim that God created by speaking because modern physics doesn't support such a claim. But here's the fantastic thing:

Hebrew is alpha**numeric**. In the beginning, God created (spoke into existence) the heavens (*shamayim*) and the earth (*erets*). Why is that significant? These letters and words undergird the spiritual dimension of Creation. Since each letter also has a numeric aspect, we could suggest that when He spoke the world into existence, God was creating the mathematical code undergirding reality (all of heaven and earth). The fact is, God's Word lines up precisely with science. We live in a mathematical universe created by God's words. This fact reminds me of the movie *The Matrix*. In it, Neo saw the letters and the numbers going down the screen revealing the basis of reality. That movie was science fiction, but there is a code to Creation. The spiritual code to Creation is His Word, which is this combination of letters and numbers. It's God's Creation Code—a spiritual DNA.

The Power of His Word

The Greek language is also alphanumeric. Hebrews 1:3 tells us that God "upholds all things by the word of His power" (NASB). Therefore, every word in the Bible has a numerical value, and the numeric values of words are often significant. While studying, when you find words with similar numeric values, you can find exciting connections, wisdom, and revelations.

An example from Scripture is the *Shema* (Deut. 6:4). It's one of the first prayers all Jewish kids learn and is the centerpiece of the daily morning and evening prayers. Some consider the *Shema* the essential prayer of Judaism. The prayer, in Hebrew, goes like this: *Shema Yisrael Adonai Eloheinu, Adonai Echad* (Hear O Israel, the Lord our God the Lord is One [*Echad*]). The word *Echad* has a numerical value of 13. How do we get to that? The first letter *Aleph* equals one, *Chet*, the second letter of the word has a numeric value of eight. And *Dalet*, the last letter equals four. When you add those together, they equal 13 (*Aleph* [1] + *Chet* [8] + *Dalet* [4] = 13). In Hebrew, thirteen is the number of oneness.

$$1 + 8 + 4 = 13$$
$$\text{OR}$$
$$\text{ALEPH + CHET + DALET} = 13$$

Let's go a bit deeper. Becoming one is rooted in love. The word for love in Hebrew is *Ahavah* and the numerical value of its letters is 13 (*Aleph* [1] + *Hei* [5] + *Bet* [2] + *Hei* [5] = 13). "One" (*Echad*) equals 13, as does "love."

$$1 + 5 + 2 + 5 = 13$$
$$\text{OR}$$
$$\text{ALEPH + HEI + BET + HEI} = 13$$

The pathway to oneness goes through love. In Western thought, 13 is a bad, unlucky number. Some hotels don't label the 13th floor because a lot of people don't want to stay on it. My first name is Jason, and on Friday the 13th people have always made all sorts of jokes.

Here's the point: in Hebrew, "13" is a blessed number.

It's the number of love and the number of oneness. It is also the number of God's "13 Attributes of Mercy" (cf. Exodus 34:6–7). We find a connection between "love" and the number 13 in the New Testament as well. 1 Corinthians 13 is the "love chapter." It has 13 verses. Why? Because this chapter is the embodiment of love.[1]

When we study letters and numbers, we make deeper connections that give us wisdom and insight into the Scripture. Our analysis begins with a basic understanding of the numerical value of each letter. We then breakdown the letters that comprise a given word. By adding up the values of those letters, we arrive at a sum total for that word.

You might be thinking to yourself: "But where does the Bible mention these important connections between letters and numbers?" Well, the answer can be found in a famous passage of Scripture.

A Well-Known Example

A biblical basis for the rich meaning in letters and numbers is in the Book of Revelation—the "Mark of the Beast." Revelation 13:18 tells us, "Here is wisdom: let the one **who has understanding calculate** the number of the beast, for it is a number of a man, and his number

....

1 The original biblical manuscripts did not have chapter and verse division. Though the chapters and verse are not inspired, I think the Holy Spirit can use them to confirm the truths in Scripture (which are!).

5

is 666." The Apostle John tells us that there is wisdom in understanding the number. The name of the beast totals 666. That's using the alphanumeric system to gain understanding.

Other biblical passages use letters and numbers to describe a concept, a person, or connection. For example, 1 Samuel 13:1-2 notes how old Saul was when he became king. If you pick up the Jewish Publication Society translation, you will read: "Saul was ... years old when he became king; and when he had reigned two years over Israel" (1 Samuel 13:1). The first sentence has a blank instead of a number.

Other Bible translations read that Saul began to rule at thirty years of age, but the number 30 is not in the original text. The Hebrew text says, "when he was *Beit nun*, meaning a son of one. Some people think that the text says that Saul was one year when he began to rule. That's a good literal translation, but realistically it can't be the case. However, if you understand Hebrew alphanumerically, then you know that *Beit nun* equals 52. The text is probably saying that Saul was fifty-two years of age when he began to reign. The letters' numerical values give us a hint at his age. This interpretation makes sense because a few verses later, we read about Saul's son Jonathan being a great warrior. How could Jonathan be an accomplished soldier if his father was only thirty years old? It doesn't seem to add up (literally).

There are many examples throughout the Bible of the significance of letters and numbers. They can give us great insight. Further, as you study the numbers, you will begin to see biblical connections you've never seen before. Most importantly, this sort of study reveals God's character—He is in the details. The Bible has a mathematical precision and a beauty to it that is astounding.

More About This Study

As we go through this journey of letters and numbers, we're going to look at each letter and its numerical value. We're going to take a deep dive into the meaning of those numbers and their meanings for us both spiritually and practically. It's thrilling to examine the numbers, see the connections, and have the proverbial light bulbs go off—those "aha" moments. I believe you are going to have those "aha" moments as well. You're going to discover greater insight into different Scripture passages and gain a fresh sense of awe at God's brilliance. I've been blessed by studying letters and numbers, and I'm sure it will bless you too!

ALEPH

א

1

The Letter *Aleph* and the Number One א

OVERVIEW

The first letter of the Hebrew alphabet is the letter *Aleph* (it's pronounced "ah-lef"). *Aleph* has no sound of its own, but usually has a vowel associated with it. *Aleph* means "chief, strength, or ruler." In some circles, *Aleph* is known as the "father" of the Hebrew *Aleph-Bet*. The original pictograph of *Aleph* represents an ox, strength, and leader.

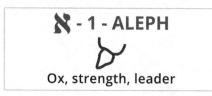

א - 1 - ALEPH

Ox, strength, leader

Aleph has a numerical value of one. This is significant because it points to the God of Israel's primary prayer, the *Shema: Shema Yisrael, Adonai Eloheinu, Adonai*

Echad, or "Hear O Israel, the Lord our God, the Lord is one" (Deut 6:4). *Aleph* is the letter representing God's oneness. And the word *echad* , which is the Hebrew word for "one," begins with an *Aleph*. It should be noted that he is the *Aleph*, and 'the *Aleph* and the *Tav*,' as in the first and the last.

Astonishingly, the shape of the letter *Aleph* reflects unity. The letters in the Hebrew alphabet are combined in different ways to create the various letters. In this case,

THREE LETTERS COMBINE TO CREATE *ALEPH*

YUD - VAV - YUD

ALEPH

three other Hebrew letters comprise the *Aleph*. There are two *yuds* (one in the upper right, and the other in the lower left, and the letter *vav* that joins them. Why is that significant? The top letter *yud* stands for the Divine Name of God, *Yud-Hey-Vav-Hey*, or YHVH (often translated "LORD" or "Jehovah" in English Bibles). The bottom letter (*yud*) stands for "*Ysrael* or Israel." The center letter, *vav*, is the letter of connection, and it looks similar to a rolled Torah scroll.

Even in the construction of the letter *Aleph* we can see that God is one. The Torah is one. God's people are one. Israel is one. The Jew and Gentile are one in Messiah.

Oneness

The letter *Aleph* and the number one remind us that:

- God is One.
- God is the only chief and only ruler.
- God is sovereign over all of creation.
- The Torah is one.
- God's people are intended to be one. Israel in the Old Testament was one nation and one people. The New Testament tells us there is one new man. It teaches that together, Jew and Gentile, form one body, and one people of God (Eph. 2:11–15).

DIGGING DEEPER

Read John 17:21, Ephesians 2:11–15, 4:3, 13 and reflect on the concept of oneness. What does it mean to you to be one with God?

_____

_____

_____

_____

_____

One is a prime number, meaning it cannot be divided. What does that tell you about God? What does that tell you about the relationship you have with God? Read Ezekiel 37:22. What does this verse tell you about "one nation" and "one people"?

_____

_____

_____

_____

_____

The Names of God

When you add up the three separate letters that form the shape of *Aleph*, they equal 26 (*Yud* [10] + *Yud* [10] + *Vav* [6] equals 26). Why is this significant? 26 is the

10 + 10 + 6 = 26
OR
YUD + YUD + VAV = 26

numerical value of the sacred name YHWH. *Aleph's* structure points to 26—the Sovereign Lord who is over all. Therefore, *Aleph* is the letter that captures and represents the name of God. Most of the names of God in the Bible begin with the letter *Aleph*. Genesis Chapter 1 says, "In the beginning God (*Elohim*) created the heavens and the earth." *Elohim*, in Hebrew, translated as God, begins with the letter *Aleph*. Here are some names of God that begin with *Aleph*:

- *Adonai*—Lord or master
- *El*—the name of God meaning "strength, might, or power."
- *Elohim*—the name of God as the Creator and Judge of the universe
- *Eloah*–God, a singular form of Elohim.
- *Adon Olam*—Eternal or Everlasting Lord
- *Ehyeh Asher Ehyeh*—I am that I am

DIGGING DEEPER

As you see, God has several names. Each one points to a different characteristic that He has. What do you discover in these names about God? Which of these names reminds you of an experience you've had with the Lord?

_____

_____

_____

_____

_____

_____

_____

_____

God's Glory

We also find that *Aleph* connects to the glory of God. Because *Aleph* א is the only letter facing towards the right, the other twenty-one letters in the Hebrew alphabet face the opposite direction. *Aleph* (in Hebraic thought) represents the oneness, the sovereignty, and the glory of God's presence. God told Moses, "you can't see my face, you can only see my back" (Ex. 33:20–23). The twenty-one other letters realize they can't look directly onto the fullness of God's glory. The other letters are turned. They, like Moses, can only see the back, which represents God's glory as well.

The children of Israel saw God's glory as He showed them mercy and grace in His deliverance of them from Egyptian bondage (Exod. 16:7, 10; 33:18–34:8; Lev 9:23; Deut. 5:24). God's glory filled the places that He subsequently designated as meeting places with His people: The Tabernacle (Exod. 40:34) and the Temple (1 Kings 8:10–11). How does God show His glory to you?

The Crown of God's Creation

The Hebrew word for "man" is *adam*. Three letters make up the word *adam*. The first letter is *Aleph*, and the second letter is *Dalet*. The third letter is *Mem*. Why is it significant that the name of the first man—"Adam"— begins with the letter *Aleph*? First, the letter *Aleph* and its characteristic of oneness remind us of God, and we need to make God our number one priority. We must understand that everything needs to revolve around Him. Adam's name should always remind us that the One who made us, our Creator, needs to be our King.

adam
FINAL MEM - DALET - ALEPH
אדם

Also, the three letters of the name of Adam are significant because, in the very beginning, God created (*bara*) the heavens (*shâmayim*), and He created the earth (*erets*). This means there are spiritual and material (or physical) components to Creation. The earth represents the physical, and heaven represents the spiritual component. When God created the first man, He made a microcosm of creation. Adam's name reflects the harmony of heaven and earth. How? The *Aleph* represents God's name, what makes man the crown of God's creation is that we are made in the image of God (*Tselem Elohim*). *Aleph* represents the image of God in us. God breathed the breath of life into us, and, in a sense, He puts part of Himself within us. His breath in us is the spiritual aspect of man, represented by the letter *Aleph*. The second two letters, the *dalet,* and *mem* of Adam spell the Hebrew word *dam*

dam

FINAL MEM - DALET

ד ם

which means "blood." When you write Adam's name, you see the *Aleph* (representing the spiritual, godly soul, God's image in man) and *dam* (representing flesh and blood). When you remove the *Aleph*, we're nothing more than animals, flesh, and blood. We're reduced to mere beasts.

DIGGING DEEPER

Read Exodus 20:3 and Matthew 6:33. The lesson is that there will always be a problem when you put anything ahead of God. What kinds of problems emerge when we put anything ahead of God?

The Difference Between Exile and Redemption

The Hebrew word for redemption is *ga-al*. The Hebrew word for exile is the word *galah*. There's only a one letter

ga-al	galah
LAMED - ALEPH - GIMEL	HE - LAMED - GIMEL
גאל	גלה

difference between these two Hebrew words: *Aleph*. What remains when you take God out of the equation? Exile. Exile is about disconnection, distance, and ultimately leads to death. When we take God out of our lives and remove Him from society and culture, it should be no surprise that we see disconnection and chaos. Disconnection leads to death and a broken, chaotic world. The world becomes *tohu*, "formless and void" when we remove the *Aleph* (God).

tohu
VAV - HE - TAV
תהו

We undo exile and move towards redemption by restoring the *Aleph*. We need to invite God back into our lives and make Him number one. Redemption will fill the earth when we do this. Zechariah 14:9 says, "ADONAI [the Lord] will then be King [*Melech*] over all the earth. In that day ADONAI will be *Echad* (One) and His Name *Echad*."

The fullness of redemption will be realized when God is one, and we are one in Him, symbolized by the letter, *Aleph*. Now, more than ever, we need to embody the *Aleph* and be one in Messiah.

DIGGING DEEPER

Read Galatians 3:13 and Ephesians 1:7. What does it mean to be redeemed and freed from exile? Is there anything that has you in exile? Declare now that Yeshua Messiah has redeemed you and freed you from anything that holds you in captivity.

_____

_____

_____

_____

_____

_____

The Alpha and the Omega

The New Testament says that Yeshua-Jesus is the "Alpha and Omega" (Rev. 1:8, 21:6, 22:13). This Greek phrase means that Jesus is the beginning and the end (*Alpha* is the first letter of the Greek alphabet, and *Omega* is the last). Hebrew is the language of The Hebrew Scriptures (*Tanakh*). Greek is the primary language of The New Testament. The Disciples, however, would have spoken

Hebrew. The Hebrew version of the Greek phrase "Alpha and Omega" would have been, "*Aleph-Tav*" **ת**–**א** because *Tav* is the last letter of the Hebrew alphabet. When we put God back into our lives, we put Jesus back in because He is *Aleph*, the top. He is the One—the beginning, and the end.

Not only is Yeshua the *Aleph* and the *Tav* in Scripture, but He also said "I am the way, the truth, and the life! No one comes to the Father except through Me. If you have come to know Me, you will know My Father also. From now on, you do know Him and have seen Him" (John 14:6–7).

The Hebrew word for truth is the word *Emet*. It's comprised of three letters. *Aleph* is the first, *mem* is the middle, and *Tav* is the last. *Emet* contains the first, mid-

> ## Emet
> ### TAV – MEM – ALEPH
> ## אמת

dle, and last letters of the Hebrew alphabet. Why is that significant? For something to be accurate, it needs to be true from the beginning to the middle to the end. But if we dig a little deeper here, there is an amazing truth waiting to be found. *Aleph* represents the name of God and Yeshua. What happens when you remove the first letter of the word truth? The word that remains is the Hebrew word for Dead (*Meit*)—the opposite of life.

Meit

TAV –MEM

מת

When you remove God (the *Aleph*), not only do you wind up with chaos, but you also ruin the truth, which ultimately culminates with death. There's a truth that brings life and shows us that Jesus is the truth and the life. There are scientific or factual truths that tell us *how* things happen, but they can't tell us *why*. These sorts of truths can't tell us why we're here. They can tell us why something happens, however, they can't tell us why we're here in our greatest pursuit for purpose and meaning in life. It's when we put the *Aleph* back in—when we make Yeshua the Chief of our life, and make Him the single priority of our life, that we find genuine Truth, life, and blessing.

DIGGING DEEPER

Read Deuteronomy 32:4 and John 8:31–32. Why is it important for you to realize that Yeshua is the Truth? How does His Truth and His Faithfulness connect and give you assurance of His promises?

Pointing to God's Oneness

Adam and Eve fell when they ate from the Tree of the Knowledge of Good and Evil. The word "to eat," or food, in Hebrew, is *akal.* So again, we find a word beginning with *Aleph.* This *Aleph* reminds us that nothing is more important than the One who made the food—*Elohim.* What happened when they relegated God to second place? They disobeyed and ate (a*kal*) from the Tree of Knowledge—the Fall. How do we reverse the curse and restore the blessing? We put God first.

As I mentioned earlier, the *Aleph* has a numerical value of one, and it points to God's oneness. Three Hebrew letters comprise the word *Aleph: Aleph, lamed,* and *peh. Peh* without the dot (dagesh) is known as the letter *feh.* It's interesting because when you total these three letters, they equal 111 (*Aleph* [1] + *lamed* [30] + *peh* [80]). *Aleph* equals one, but when you total the letters, they equal 111. Why is that significant? Because God is the God of the ones. He's also the God of the tens.

$$1 + 30 + 80 = 111$$
$$\text{OR}$$
$$\text{ALEPH} + \text{LAMED} + \text{PEH} = 111$$

He's the God of the hundreds. And the word *Aleph* in Hebrew can also be 1,000. The numbers teach us, that while God has many names, He is the One who holds it all together, from the smallest atom to the greatest element. He is the One who is Lord of it all. He is the One who brought everything into existence. It is stunning how this letter, *Aleph*, points to God and the Oneness of God. From the largest to tiniest details, the Lord is the Creator, and the Lord is the King.

DIGGING DEEPER

Read Matthew 22:37 and Romans 11:33–36. "**God** is indeed the Sovereign of all things, the One to whom all creatures are accountable and whom all should glorify."[1] What does the declaration that God is "Lord of it all" mean for your daily life? Is this something that encourages you? Does it challenge you?

_____

_____

_____

_____

_____

_____

_____

....

1 John A. Witmer, "Romans," in *The Bible Knowledge Commentary: An Exposition of the Scriptures*, ed. J. F. Walvoord and R. B. Zuck, vol. 2 (Wheaton, IL: Victor Books, 1985), 487.

Aleph, Genesis, and Six

When we read Genesis 1:1, there are six *Alephs*. Why is it important? The six *Alephs* represent the six days of

Genesis 1:1

בְּרֵאשִׁית בָּרָא אֱלֹהִים אֵת הַשָּׁמַיִם וְאֵת הָאָרֶץ

God's work of creation. Scripture says that one day with the Lord is like 1,000 years (2 Peter 3:8). From a Jewish, more in-depth perspective, the six *Alephs* reveal the Jewish tradition that the world can only exist 6,000 years before the Messiah comes to establish His Kingdom. We're in the decade of 5,780 on the biblical calendar, the last days of that 6,000-year era. God created the heavens and the earth in six days and rested on the seventh. This world, and our life experience, is like six days. During these "six days" we prepare and work. Then, on the seventh day, we will rest. In traditional Jewish thought, Messiah has to come by the year 6,000 establishing His Kingdom and bringing Sabbath—the world will then rest for 1,000 years.

Yeshua will come to establish the Kingdom of God on earth as it is in heaven. Several exciting thoughts are embodied in the letter *Aleph* as it relates to 1,000. Recall, *Aleph* means "ruler or king." Also, the Hebrew word *Melech* implies king. What is the difference between an *Aleph* chief, leader, or ruler and a *Melech* king? In Jewish thought, an *Aleph* leader or ruler might be a lord or master but is not acknowledged or crowned king. An *Aleph* ruler or leader is king in name only, but not in authority or rulership. *Melech* is a crowned king. All people recognize them, and all people pay homage to the *Melech*. He is a king who is in the position of rulership and leadership. Why is that significant? Because in a sense, God is *Melech* among His people. He's the King among believers, but he's not the *Melech* of the world because the world hasn't yet recognized Him as the only true King, Creator, and Redeemer.

Recall Zechariah 14:9 that says the Lord will be One, and His name will be One. God's name will be One only when there's the complete revelation of Him in the world. At that time, "at the name of Yeshua every knee should bow, in heaven and on the earth and under the earth, and every tongue profess that Yeshua the Messiah is Lord—to the glory of God the Father" (Phil 2:10-11).

Then, He will be recognized as both the *Aleph* and the *Melech*, the true king, who will reign for 1,000 years. He will be acknowledged and worshiped. It's at that moment all the people will go up to Jerusalem, symbolizing the conclusion of 6,000 years, and commence the Sabbath (1,000 years) with all the nations worshiping and adoring Him.

The Power of God

The letter *Aleph* also connects to the power of God. When you read the word *Aleph* backward, it spells the Hebrew word *pele,* meaning "miracles, wonderful, or marvelous." Why is that detail relevant? Because the *Aleph* represents Messiah. He is the One, the *Aleph*, at the top of all things. *Pele* is one of the titles for the Messiah. Isaiah 9:6 says, "For to us a child is born, a son will be given to us, and the government will be upon His shoulder. His Name will be called Wonderful [*pele*] Counselor, Mighty God My Father of Eternity, Prince of Peace." In this verse, we find *Aleph* spelled backward. The *Aleph* points to Messiah because he is the true Lord and true King. He is the one sent by the Father.

Friends, we need to understand that because God is One, we are called to be one in Him and make Him "one" in our lives. We need to invite Him back into the central place in our culture, believing this shift will lead to life, blessing, and the truth going forth.

DIGGING DEEPER

Read Isaiah 29:29 and Matthew 28:18. What does the phrase "miraculously wonderful" tell you about Yeshua? How would you like to see the Messiah's miraculously wonderful power demonstrated in your life?

_____

_____

_____

_____

_____

SUMMARY

- The letter *Aleph* is the first letter of the Hebrew alphabet. It also represents the number one (and also 10, 100, and 1000).
- *Aleph* represents the Oneness of God. It connotes "leader, master, Lord."
- The parts of the letter *Aleph* ad up to 26. This is the same as the sacred name YHVH. This also indicates a connection between *Aleph* and the LORD.
- *Aleph* is the first letter of many of God's names
- Yeshua is the *Aleph* and the *Tav*

What part of this lesson had the most impact on you? Why?

The Letter *Bet* and the Number Two ב

OVERVIEW

The letter *bet* (it rhymes with "mate") is the second letter of the Hebrew alphabet. It has the sound of "b" as in "bread" or "boy." It has a numerical value of two, and the Hebrew word *Bayit*, which means "house" relates to the letter *bet*. Early pictographs of the letter look something like a house with the left-side opening appearing as a window.

ב - 2 - BET
⌂
House, family, in

The First Word of the Bible

The first words of the Hebrew Bible begin, *beresheet bara*. This is noteworthy because the first letter of the entire

Bible isn't *Aleph*, but the letter *Bet*. The rabbis questioned, "Why didn't God begin the Torah [the five books of Moses] with the letter *Aleph*?" The rabbis pondered this because it seemed reasonable to them that the first word of the Hebrew Scriptures should start with the first letter of their alphabet, the *Aleph*.

I think this question matters for two reasons:

- First, *Bet* has a numerical value of two. God created the world in twos. He created the heavens and the earth. The number two points to the dual aspect of heavens above and the earth below. Two refers to the physical and spiritual parts of creation.

- Second, and perhaps more meaningful, the last word of the New Testament book of Revelation is the Hebrew word, "*amen.*" The last letter of *amen* is the Hebrew letter *Nun* (pronounced "noon"). When you combine the Bible's first letter in Genesis, *Bet*, and the last letter from Revelation, *Nun*, it spells the Hebrew word, **Ben** which means "son." From the first letter of the Bible to the last letter, we find the word, "son." Why? Because from beginning to end, everything in the Bible points to the Son, Jesus, Messiah.

There's another reason the Bible begins with the letter *Bet*. Yeshua is the second person of the Godhead, who created everything. He is the Son (*Ben*) of God. When we dig a bit deeper, we find there's more about this link between *Bet* and the Son. The preposition "in" is another function of *Bet*. Genesis 1:1, "In the beginning" in Hebrew is written with the letter *Bet*. Essentially, the letter *Bet* can be attached to the beginning of a word, and it becomes the preposition "in." Why does this matter? Because when you look at the letter *Bet*, in the middle of the white space, there is a round dot known as a *dagesh* (Hebrew for "mark"). The white space in the letter and the *dagesh* are symbolic of the world existing *in* God. As Paul said

VET | BET WITH DAGESH
ב | בּ

when he addressed the Areopagus, "In Him, we live and move and have our being" (Acts 17:28). Paul proclaimed God as the Creator and the Source of Creation, and life is found in the *Ben*, the Son. Apart from the Son, there is no eternal or lasting life. The world is found in Him, and to find life, we need to be found in Him.

DIGGING DEEPER

Read Psalm 119:105. God's Word is a lamp. It's not a broad searchlight, however, but more like a focused lamp or flashlight. Scripture illuminates Yeshua and the path

He has for each of us. In what ways does knowing that the *Ben* (the Son) is found in every word of the Bible keep you focused on God's promises, provision, and path?

_____

_____

_____

_____

_____

_____

_____

Read John 5:26. What does it mean to you "even as the Father has life within Himself, so the Son has that life within Himself, and power to give life?" How has your life demonstrated Yeshua's power to give life?

_____

_____

_____

_____

_____

_____

Two Biblical Worlds

The letter *Bet*, the first letter of the Bible, points to two worlds biblically. In Hebraic thought, God created not one world but two. First, there is this world, which in

Hebrew, is called *Olam-Ha-Zeh*. The second world which is called *Olam ha-Ba* is to come when the Messiah returns and establishes His Kingdom. This second word begins with the letter *Bet*.

In Matthew 23:39, Jesus said, "For I tell you, you will never see Me again until you say, '*Baruch ha-Ba B'shem* ADONAI. Blessed is He who comes in the name of the Lord!'" The words *Bara* ("bless"), *ha-Ba* ("comes"), and *b'shem* ("the name of the Lord") all begin with a *Bet*. Why? because there's this world, and then there is the world to come. The letter *Bet* primarily focuses on the coming of the *Ben*, the Son, who brings the life in this world and the world to come.

In traditional Jewish thought, all of time is broken up into these two perspectives—these two worlds. The world to come is the Kingdom of God—the new heavens and the new earth. These concepts have implications for us because in this world we now prepare for the world to come. Yeshua said, "We must do the work of the One who sent Me, so long as it is day! Night is coming when no one can work" (John 9:4). God calls us to be two-world people. Many people merely live for this world. We, believers in Yeshua, are called to live for the world to come. We're not physical beings having a spiritual experience. We're spiritual beings having a physical experience. Our worldview is shaped by our understanding that this present world is a time of preparation for the world to come.

DIGGING DEEPER

Read Luke 13:18–30. "Jesus pictured the kingdom as a great feast, with the patriarchs and prophets as honored guests (Luke 13:28). But many of the people who were invited waited too long to respond; and, when they arrived at the banquet hall, it was too late and the door was shut (see Matt. 22:1–14; Luke 14:15–24)."[1] Why did they wait so long? Do you think they were preparing for the Kingdom in this life?

_____

_____

_____

_____

_____

_____

God's Dwelling Place

As I mentioned in the overview, *Bet* (in its appearance) and the Hebrew word *Bayit* mean a house. This meaning goes directly to God's underlying motivation for creating the universe. He desired a dwelling place below like His dwelling place above. God wanted to create a dwelling place, a house that He could fill with family because God is love. When you love, you naturally want to share it. Love is outwardly focused. This is why men and women

....
1 Warren W. Wiersbe, *The Bible Exposition Commentary*, vol. 1 (Wheaton, IL: Victor Books, 1996), 226.

get married and have children. The *Bet* represents the house, and the house represents God's plan to fill that house with family. Yeshua said, "In My Father's house there are many dwelling places. If it were not so, would I have told you that I am going to prepare a place for you?" (John 14:2) The *Bet* symbolizes the house that Yeshua the Messiah is preparing for you and me.

Bayit, is also the name for the house of God, The Temple in Jerusalem. I love taking people to Israel. Jerusalem is my favorite place to go during Our Rock Road Rabbit Israel tours. In Jerusalem, my favorite site to visit is the Western Wall, which is part of the *Har Habayit,* the Temple Mount. This is the location of the Temple that Solomon built and the Second Temple where Yeshua worshiped—in the *Bayit,* God's house, or the *Bet HaMikdash.* The Temple is God's holy house, His holy sanctuary. Quoting several Old Testament prophets, Yeshua said, "Is it not written, 'My house shall be called a house of prayer for all the nations?'" Matthew 21:13). God takes His house seriously.

Of course, there's more. *Bet* represents the number two and *Bayit* means "house." This reminds us of two of the houses of worship in Israel's history: the Temple built by Solomon and the other completed by King Herod. Both of those glorious Temples tie back to God's purpose for creation. This first letter in Genesis signifies that the Lord wants a dwelling place below, on earth, like He has in heaven. This means that God created the world so that He could dwell with us—be in a relationship and connected with us. This is the ultimate reason God sent His Spirit. And it's so interesting, because the *Bet*, the *bayit*, or the *Bet HaMikdash* foreshadowed God's people as His dwelling place. In Exodus 25:8, God said to Moses, "Have them make a Sanctuary for Me, so that I may dwell among them." The Hebrew word for "among them" is *betocham* which can either mean "among them" or "within each of them," but it begins with the letter *Bet*. God initially dwelt "among" the children of Israel—*betocham*. The *Bet* and the *bayit* are represented by the second letter of the Hebrew alphabet. Ultimately, that was stage one—to draw *betocham* in the *Bet HaMikdash,* in the house that is made with human hands. Eventually however, what God wants to do is not to dwell among us, but to dwell *in* us. He wants you to become His *bayit*. The letter *Bet* with the *dagesh* (dot) is a picture of the Holy Spirit dwelling in us

VET | BET

ב בּ

at the center of our lives. Paul wrote in Colossians 1:27, "God chose to make known to them this glorious mystery regarding the Gentiles—which is Messiah in you, the hope of glory!" We can be in the Son and have God's Spirit dwelling in us as His dwelling place. Ephesians 3:16 tells us, "I pray that from His glorious riches He would grant you to be strengthened in your inner being with power through His *Ruach* [Spirit]." God wants us to know the riches of His glory, the glory of Messiah. Knowing the riches of His Glory is our assurance of sharing in His glory.

DIGGING DEEPER

Read Colossians 3:11 and John 14:17. The glorious mystery of God is that Messiah will come and indwell you. How does His indwelling cause you to have a life of fellowship with God? What does living after the indwelling Spirit mean to you? How does it shape your walk with God?

_____

_____

_____

_____

_____

_____

Bet is the Letter of Blessing

Earlier, I shared two reasons why *Bet* was the first letter of the Bible. I want to share another reason: the letter *Bet* is the letter of blessing. In the Hebrew text of Genesis 1, the first *Bet* is written with an enlarged letter *Bet* ב. The Hebrew word for blessing is *berakah* in the singular and *berakhot* in the plural.

Genesis begins with the letter *Bet* and not with *Aleph*, because the letter *Aleph* is the first letter of the Hebrew word for cursing, *arar*. Genesis 3:17 says, "Then to the man He said, 'Because you listened to your wife's voice and ate of the tree which I commanded you, saying, 'You must not eat of it': Cursed [*arar*] is the ground because of you—with pain will you eat of it all the days of your life.'" God wanted to make it abundantly clear that the world was not created for cursing, but His intention, motivation, and heart were to create the world for blessing. You are created to be blessed! This is why the letter *Bet* has the dot in the center—it represents God filling His house (*bayit*) with His blessings (*berakhot*). God wants to fill your house and your life with blessings. He doesn't want to bring cursing but a life overflowing with blessings.

Blessing is connected to the number two and it is crucial that we understand the implications of this. Blessing and the number two are not connected only because *Bet* is the first letter of the Hebrew word blessing—there's something more. Remember, the letter *Bet* symbolizes God creating the world in twos. He created heaven and earth. He also created day and night. He created light and darkness. He created the sea and dry land. He created the six days of the week to work, and the seventh day the *Shabbat*, the day for resting. He created man, but man wasn't complete until God brought forth woman. What's the point? The fullness of God's blessing only appears when the two opposites come into alignment and partner together. We need the proper balance of light and darkness, or there is no life. Without the appropriate balance of sun and rain, we don't have crops or food to eat. Until a man and woman come together, they can't be fruitful and multiply. Without the proper relationship between the two, the first commandment—to be fruitful and multiply (*cf* Gen 1:28)—cannot be realized.

DIGGING DEEPER

Read Isaiah 40:12 and Proverbs 8:22–31. We find God's wisdom and splendor everywhere in creation. God created so many aspects of the world and universe. How does creating things in twos demonstrate God's wisdom? Working with a person with an opposite personality or strengths from our own can be challenging, yet beneficial. What benefits have you seen working or living with someone who has different strengths than you?

Establishing a House Aligned

When the two come into alignment, that's when the *berakah* (blessing) develops and the *Bayit*, the house, is established. In the same way that God created man and woman, He created Jew and Gentile. The Bible separates all of humanity into Israel and the nations—into Jew and Gentile. However, God's creational purpose is only realized when the two become one. Yeshua prayed, "that they [those who believe in Him] all may be one. Just as You, Father, are in Me and I am in You, so also may they be one in Us, so the world may believe that You sent Me" (John 17:21). He also said, "I in them and You in Me—that they may be perfected in unity, so that the world may know that You sent Me and loved them as You loved Me" (John 17:23). The world will not know He is the One until the two (man and woman, Jew and Gentile, etc.) become one in Him. Paul wrote about this in Ephesians 2:13–14, "But now in Messiah Yeshua, you who once were far off have been brought near by the blood of the Messiah. For He is our shalom, the One who made the two into one and broke down the middle wall of separation."

This concept of unity is what our ministry, Fusion Global, is all about. When there is a fusion—a coming together of Jew and Gentile, of Word and Spirit—it releases the fullness of God's blessing. If you want to receive the *berakah* (blessing), it's found in the coming together of old and new, Jew and Gentile. This connection is the Kingdom oneness we discussed in Chapter 1. Are you seeking oneness in Messiah as well as in other relationships?

On a practical level, this oneness includes embracing the Jewish roots of the faith, yet it also involves Kingdom alignments in your relationships. Are you unified in relationship with the people you're supposed to be walking with? Is your family living in unity? It's critical to see relational unity and alignment at work because alignment leads to blessing! Alignment and unity are essential to experiencing breakthroughs and the fruitfulness of creation. Ultimately, two are better than one. If one falls down, the other one is there to pick them up.

SUMMARY

From the first letter to the last, all of Scripture points to the *Ben*. Let's review the words that begin with the letter *Bet*:

- *Ben*—"Son"
- *Bara*—"to create"
- *Banah*—"to build"
- *Barach*—"to bless"

Creation (*berea*) was created (*bara*) and built (*banah*) through the Son (*Ben*) with insight and discernment (*binah*) so that we might experience the blessings (*berakah*) of God in this world and in the world to come.

What part of this lesson had the most impact on you? Why?

_____

_____

_____

_____

_____

_____

_____

_____

_____

_____

_____

_____

_____

The Letter *Gimmel* and the Number Three א

OVERVIEW

The third letter of the Hebrew alphabet is called *Gimmel* (pronounced "geeh-mel"). It has the sound of "g" as in great. *Gimmel* has a numerical value of three. When we look at the image of the letter, there's profound symbolism. First, the letter is in the shape of a foot, more specifically, a person who is walking or in motion. *Gimmel* represents a wealthy person pursuing or walking after a needy person in order to provide for their needs or bless them (Hebrew, *tzedakah*, or charity*)*.

God's Magnificent Kindness and Bountiful Blessing

The Hebrew letter *Gimmel* is rooted in the Hebrew word *gāmal* (meaning "to deal fully or adequately with,

deal out to, wean or ripen"), which has the same consonant root (*Gimmel–Mem–Lamed* / גמל). In Hebrew, as
in other Semitic languages (for example Arabic and Ara-
maic), there are root words. These roots are a sequence of
consonants, typically three consonants form a root. From
these roots actual words are formed by adding vowels and
additional consonants following a specific pattern. *Gimmel* represents God's magnificent kindness and bountiful
blessing in our lives. We see this in the book of Psalms.
Psalm 13:6 says, "I will sing unto the LORD, because he
hath dealt bountifully with me" (KJV). The word translated "bountifully" is *gamal* which shares the same Hebrew
root as the Hebrew word, "*Gimmel*."[1] *Gimmel* represents
God's beneficent kindness towards us.

The letter also connects to wealth because *Gamal* is
also the Hebrew word for camel. The first time we read
about camels in the Bible is in the book of Genesis. When
Abraham sent his servant, Eliezer, to secure a wife for his
son, Isaac, he also sent ten camels (Gen. 24:10) laden with
all sorts of blessing. Abraham sent camels with riches
and treasures to be a blessing and show what a great family the prospective bride would be marrying into if she
accepted the proposal. *Gimmel* and camels are associated
with kindness, blessing, and wealth.

....

1 Hebrew letters can be written-out in long-form in addition to their symbol
(e.g. the English equivalent might be "s" or "ess").

DIGGING DEEPER

Read Luke 12:34 and 2 Corinthians 8:9. Different cultures measured wealth in different ways. In today's world, what word or phrase describes wealth and blessing? How does today's concept of wealth and blessing differ from Yeshua's definition of wealth? How has the wealth that only Yeshua offers affected your daily life?

_____

_____

_____

_____

Creating a Connecting Bridge

Gimmel is also associated with the word *gesher*, the Hebrew word for "bridge." When two pieces of land are separated, a bridge is the connecting point; the third "line" connecting the two points. *Gimmel* is associated with bridging the gap, making a connection, and creating a source of blessing.

Gimmel
represents the
bridge between
the two

| SPIRITUAL WORLD | | MATERIAL WORLD |

Reason: Torah and Spirit given in
the third month to bridge the gap.
Yeshua rises on the third day.

DIGGING DEEPER

Read Romans 3:23 and John 17:3. God sent Yeshua to bridge the separation between God and us. He paid the penalty for our sin. How have you seen Yeshua bridge the gap between you and God?

_____

_____

_____

_____

_____

_____

The Godhead, Creation, and the Number "3"

The numerical value of *Gimmel* is three. Remember the first verse of Genesis: *Beriesheet Bara Elohim* is In the beginning God created. God created the world out of nothing. The phrase "create out of nothing" is the Hebrew word, *Bara*. "This verb is of profound theological significance, since it has only God as its subject. Only God can "create" in the sense implied by *bara*. The verb expresses creation out of nothing."[2] Three letters form *Bara*: *Bet* ב, *Resh* ר, and *Aleph* א. Why is this significant? Because these three letters allude to the three Persons of the Triune Godhead involved in creation. The letter *Bet* represents

....

2 W. E. Vine, Merrill F. Unger, and William White Jr., *Vine's Complete Expository Dictionary of Old and New Testament Words* (Nashville, TN: T. Nelson, 1996), 51.

Ben, the Son. *Resh* represents the *Ruach,* the Spirit (*Ruach Kodesh* is the Holy Spirit's name in Hebrew). *Aleph* represents the *Av* or *Abba,* Father. The Father, Son, and Spirit were all involved in creation. Genesis reveals the threefold action of God. Since *Gimmel* has the numeric value of three, it represents the divine agency in creation.

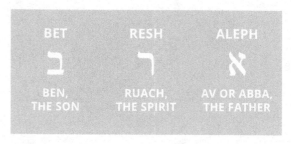

It's also significant that, as we said, the *Aleph* represents the *Av* and has a numerical value of one; the *Bet* means the Son and has a numerical value of two. And the *Gimmel* represents the *Ruach,* the Holy Spirit, and has a numerical value of three. We see that the gift of the Spirit connects to both the Father and the Son. We read about this connection in John 15:26:

> *"When the Helper comes—whom I*
> *[Yeshua-Jesus] will send to you from the Father,*
> *the Spirit of truth who goes out from the*
> *Father—He will testify about Me."*

The Father (*Aleph*)—through His Son (*Bet*)—gives the Spirit (*Gimmel*) as the greatest gift of the redeemed life.

DIGGING DEEPER

Read John 1:1–3 and Acts 17:24. The key is Yeshua. John tells us how He created the world. Jesus was with God and He was God. Along with the Holy Spirit, they created the world. How is your faith strengthened by knowing this truth?

_____

_____

_____

_____

_____

Magnificent Kindness

The sending of the Holy Spirit is a sign of God's magnificent kindness in our life. Remember, *Gimmel* represents a person who is walking or in motion. More specifically, it signifies someone moving toward us, empowering us for the work God has called us to do, running after the things of God (see Psalm 23:6 or Romans 2:4).

Gimmel points to giving to those that are in need. When the Spirit of God is present, there is always a spirit of generosity. We can find this truth in the Bible in several places:

- In Acts 2:44–45, the believers sold everything when the Spirit came, and they gave to
  anyone who had a need.
- In Exodus 36:5, the Spirit's presence was
  manifest as the children of Israel to build the
  Tabernacle. Moses told the people to stop
  giving because they had "much more than
  enough" of what they needed.

Wherever the Spirit is, there is a spirit of generosity. This spirit is related to the letter *Gimmel,* which is
the first letter of *Gamal,* "God's magnificent kindness."
Divine generosity releases an outpouring of His blessing
that empowers us to walk forward and do God's work.

DIGGING DEEPER

Read Genesis 13:19 and Romans 12:10. How do you define kindness? In what ways has God shown His magnificent kindness to you?

_____

_____

_____

_____

_____

_____

_____

Three: Peace, Oneness, and Unity

The letter *Gimmel* is the number three. It is associated with a bridge (*gesher*), which symbolizes connection and unity. Ephesians 4:3 says, "making every effort to keep the unity of the *Ruach* [Spirit] in the bond of *shalom* [the bond of peace]." In this verse, the Spirit—who is associated with the number three as the third member of the Trinity (and consequently the letter *Gimmel*)—brings the bond of peace. It's the Spirit that makes Jew and Gentile one in Messiah. Ephesians continues, "There is one body and one *Ruach*, just as you also were called in one hope of your calling; one Lord, one faith, one immersion; one God and Father of all, who is over all and through all and in all" (Ephesians 4:4–6). It is the Spirit of God that brings oneness and unity.

Three: God Created the World with Words

A figurative translation of the Hebrew in Genesis 1:1 reads, "When God spoke the world into existence." The Hebrew language is the language of creation and the language for most of the Bible. Even though the New Testament was written in Greek, it is steeped in Hebraic thought. Hebrew words are built on a trilateral root system. They are made of three letters that are related to a "root" meaning with other words of the same root. Incredibly, the Triune Godhead who created the world did so using a language that's built on a trilateral root system. In this way the Hebrew

48

language points to the nature and essence of the Creator. In the Hebrew alphabet there are twenty-two letters and five "final letters" (They have a different form when written at the end of a word). The Hebrew alphabet is broken up into sets of three (27 letters: 9 letters in each group).

ט ח ז ו ה ד ג ב א

ס ן נ מ ם ל כ ך י

ת ש ר ק ץ פ ף ע

As we learned in Chapter 1, the first letter is *Aleph*. The second letter is *Bet*. The third letter is *Gimmel*. When you take *Aleph* (one) and *Bet* (two), then add, *Gimmel* (three), that equals six. Then divide six by three; the answer is two (*Bet*). When you do this, the answer always points to the middle letter. Why is that so significant? Because everything points back to the Son, who is the second person of the Godhead. Even the Hebrew alphabet, the way it's structured, glorifies the second Person of the Godhead.

1 + 2 + 3 = 6
OR
ALEPH + (BET) + GIMMEL = 6

6 ÷ 3 = 2 (BET)

BET: the 2nd letter in this set of 3.
THE SON: the 2nd person of the godhead

DIGGING DEEPER

Read Hebrews 11:3. Nothing means "**no thing**." Before God created the world there was no energy, no gravity, no laws, no physical properties. There was "**no thing**." What thoughts do you think when you look into the night sky and see stars or look at a beautiful flower in full bloom?

_____

_____

_____

_____

_____

Three: Creation

We find the number three in the process of creation: thought, speech, and action. There's a threefold nature to how the creation of the world developed. In Jewish thought, the world stands on three priorities: The Torah, worship, and deeds of kindness. Notice the third priority is *gemilut hasadim* which begins with *Gimmel* or the word *Gamal*, to deal bountifully with deeds of kindness.

But there's more! Body, soul, and spirit form a

human. The essence of the self—body, soul, and spirit—reflects the threefold nature of the Godhead. When God chose to birth the Jewish people, how many patriarchs were there? Three—Abraham, Isaac, and Jacob (*Avraham, Yitzchak,* and *Yaakov*). The number three

(*Gimmel*) connects to the birth of Israel and the Jewish people. In a more profound sense, what this represents is that God didn't choose the Jewish people. He birthed the Jewish people, and used the three patriarchs to birth them into a nation.

DIGGING DEEPER

Read Genesis 1:13. The third day was the day the earth emerged from the water. What does this symbolize in the life of Yeshua? Do you see the connection between the number three and the Divine?

_____

_____

_____

_____

_____

_____

Three: God's Revelation

Creation is centered around the number three, but the same is true of God's revelation and the number three. According to the biblical calendar, God came down at Mount Sinai on the third day, in the third month (*cf.* Exodus 19–20). God gave the Torah through Moses, who was the third-born in his family (a little brother to Aaron and Miriam). The Hebrew Bible (*Tanakh*) is comprised of three parts or sections: the *Torah* (books of Moses), the *Nevi'im* (Prophets), and the *Kethuvim* (Writings). The revelation of the Scripture and how it came forth at Mount Sinai in its structure is centered around the number three. Three days a week in synagogues, Jewish people read publicly from a handwritten *Torah* scroll known as a *Sefer Torah*.

And there's more! The same applies to the New Testament. It contains the Gospels, the epistles (themselves made up in a three-fold structure—the Pauline epistles, Hebrews, and the general epistles), and the book of Revelation, the End Times book of the Bible.

Remember, the number three also points to the *Ruach*, the Holy Spirit. It is the Holy Spirit's role to illuminate (reveal) the Scriptures for us as part of the blessing of following Yeshua. John 14:26 says, "But the Helper, the *Ruach ha-Kodesh* [the Holy Spirit] whom the Father will send in My name, will teach you everything and remind you of everything that I said to you." The third person of the Godhead is the one who illuminates the Scripture for us to remember and apply. As Rabbi Paul told Timothy, "All scripture is God breathed" (2 Tim. 3:16). Incredibly, even the inspiration of Scripture connects to the Holy Spirit.

DIGGING DEEPER

Read 1 Corinthians 2:11–13. We come to know the things of God by His Spirit. How has the Holy Spirit opened your eyes and heart to study His Word in its fullness? How has He brought understanding that you could apply to your daily life?

_____

_____

_____

_____

_____

Three: Redemption

We've learned how the number three connects to creation and revelation, now let's discover how three connects to redemption. From a traditional Jewish understanding, when God brought the ten plagues (Ex. 7–12) upon Egypt, they were broken into three sets. Aaron initiated three plagues, Moses initiated three, and God initiated three. The plague of the boils came through all three as they partnered and worked together to produce it.

During the Passover, which celebrates the great redemption from Egypt, we spill drops of wine on three different occasions to remind us of what God did for us, and we recite the Passover story. There are also three pieces of *matzah* (unleavened bread) at the Passover Seder. It's the middle piece of *matzah* that is broken, which connects to Yeshua being broken for us and what He did at the Passover meal.

Of course, there is more as Yeshua comes as the greater than Moses and the greater Passover Lamb who brings about a greater redemption.

- Yeshua performed a miracle at the wedding of Cana of Galilee (John 2), and He performed the miracle on the third day of the week.

- Yeshua's trial was separated into two stages: three in a Jewish court and three in a Roman court (various Gospel accounts).

- Peter denied the Lord three times (Matt. 26:69–75).

- Yeshua prayed three times in the garden (Matt. 26:36–39, 42–44; Luke 22:43–44)

- There were three crosses (Luke 23:33).

- Yeshua was on the cross, crucified at the third hour. On the cross, He experienced three hours of darkness on the cross (Luke 23:44–45).

- Yeshua was raised on the third day in partial fulfillment of Hosea's prophecy which says, "Come, let us return to ADONAI. For He has torn, but He will heal us. He has smitten, but He will bind us up. After two days He will re-vive us. On the third day He will raise us up, and we will live in His presence" (Hos. 6:1–2).

- When Yeshua raised the cup at the Passover meal, the Last Supper, He raised the third cup, which is known as the cup of redemption. This reminds us of the blood of the Passover lamb, because there were three sprinklings on the top into the two sides of the doorpost on the homes of Egypt. It makes sense that He raised the third cup, because He is the Lamb of God who would spill His blood for you and me redeeming us and setting us free.

So much of what Yeshua did for our redemption is linked to the number three. His death, burial, and resurrection is the foundation for a greater redemption, the greater Exodus that we can experience in Him. He sets us free!

Read Exodus 6:2–7, Mark 10:45, and 1 Corinthians 6:19–20. The Hebrew word *ga'al* means "to redeem." Notice it begins with *Gimmel*. The very essence of redemption is to purchase something back that had been lost by payment of ransom. Yeshua paid our debt in full. He delivered His people like the greater than Moses. What new insights do you have about the concept of redemption as you read these passages?

_____

_____

_____

_____

Speaking Again of Camels

Let's examine another level with Yeshua and the *Gimmel*. He said in Matthew, "Again I tell you, it is easier for a camel to go through the eye of a needle, than for a rich man to enter the kingdom of God" (Matt. 19:24). From a Hebrew understanding, God made the letter *Gimmel* king over wealth. As we've already learned, *Gimmel* is associated with the *Gamal* (the camel); they're the same. They share the same consonant. Therefore, when Yeshua said it was easier for a camel to go through the eye of the needle, He was using the camel as a picture of wealth, and the king of wealth.

Remember, the Bible connects wealth and camels. Throughout the Scriptures (even in the End Times!) a nation's wealth is measured by camels. The letter *Gimmel* is associated with the promise of abundance and with the promise of blessing. It reminds us of God dealing bountifully with us. It's an image of God's generosity, a picture of God's eternal, beneficent kindness in our lives. The world simply cannot exist without God's loving-kindness. Much like a camel's endurance in the desert, giving wealth to the poor sustains them, even in the most barren places.

Yeshua used the camel to represent the rich man because in Hebraic thought, and throughout the Bible, the camel is a picture of wealth. It makes logical sense why He would use the idea of a camel in this parable, but Yeshua had another reason.

Yeshua used this camel and wealth association from His personal life experience. When Yeshua was a child, His family was poor. When He was born, they had no place to stay. According to Christian tradition, three wise men came from the East bearing three gifts. These gifts of wealth and generosity arrived riding on camels which was the most popular mode of transportation over long distances in that day. They brought wealth that sustained the family and allowed them to be able to flourish. In the parable, perhaps Yeshua was saying, "Just like kindness and generosity were extended to me, we need to serve other people."

The camel going through the eye of the needle is a representation of the rich man chasing after the poor man. Another dimension of Yeshua's parable is that the rich need not only to be generous, but dependent. They need to be willing to leave everything to follow Yeshua. He provides us with the account of the rich young ruler whom Yeshua directed to sell everything and then return and follow Him. The rich man went away sad because he had many possessions that he wasn't willing to give up. We must leave everything for the sake of the call. Yeshua is saying it's easier for those who have nothing to follow Him and it's harder for those who have everything to lay it all down and follow Him. Sometimes you need to leave everything at the feet of the King. That's what God calls every one of us to do. Our obedience marks us out as His followers and heirs of the eternal life that He promised.

DIGGING DEEPER

Read Matthew 6:19–21 and Luke 12:14–15. Can you recall an experience in your life, or in the life of someone you know, in which hoarding led to loss rather than to increase or blessing of others? What was the final effect? In the Talmud, it is said that the *Gimmel* symbolizes a rich man running after a poor man to serve him or give him a blessing. Why do you think serving and giving a blessing is so connected to Yeshua's message?

_____

_____

_____

_____

_____

SUMMARY

Three is the number of strength—a threefold cord cannot be broken. The nuclear family—mom, dad, and children—is threefold. This substantive family cord provides strength for every society. The family has the potential to serve as a "social bedrock" with the strength of that threefold cord. This cord also holds a biblical community or a spiritual family together. God's spiritual family entails three "cords" coming together—Jew and Gentile, centered around the person of Yeshua. He is the bridge and we are united in Him.

How do we respond to this revelation of God's Triune essence in so many aspects of nature and society? Is it not mind-blowing to see these supernatural signposts pointing us to the Son? God has generously revealed Himself to us! We must respond by dealing bountifully with others. As we bless others, we will experience yet another level of God's blessing in our lives.

Gimmel reveals a rich man running after a poor man to bless him. Friends, we don't run after riches. We run after the Lord, and we run to be a blessing to those in need. "I will sing to the Lord because he has done bountifully with me" (Psa. 13:6). May you be generous and gracious and be a source of blessing to many others.

What was most important to you in this lesson about *Gimmel*? Why?

_____

_____

_____

_____

_____

DALET
ד
4

The Letter *Dalet* and the Number Four ד

OVERVIEW

Dalet (pronounced dah-let) is the fourth letter of the Hebrew alphabet, and like many of the letters has meaning and symbolism. It has the sound of "d" as in "door"— The Hebrew word for door is *delet*. *Dalet* has a numeric value of four. The *Dalet* is a picture of an open door. The

letter also represents a poor person that is bent over begging or asking for help. These two concepts combine as *Dalet* represents a poor person going to a home, seeking help. They find an open door and someone who is willing to provide for them in their need.

Dalet and Gimmel

There is a significant connection between the *Gimmel* ג (the third letter) and the *Dalet*. You will recall from our last lesson that the *Gimmel* represents the wealthy person. The *Dalet* represents the poor person. These two letters give us an image of the wealthy person chasing after the poor person to be a blessing. We see a picture of this relationship in Genesis 18:1–21, which notes that Abraham saw some wayfarers in need. He ran to prepare food for them, not aware that he was entertaining angels. And God poured out a blessing on him for his kindness. Proverbs 19:17 reminds us, "One who is kind to the poor lends to ADONAI, and ADONAI will reward him for his good deed." The Hebrew word for "poor" in this verse is *dal* and begins with a *dalet*. Furthermore, the Hebrew word for "reward" is *Gamal*, which, as we learned in lesson three, also means "to deal bountifully." The Lord would deal bountifully with Abraham for his good deeds. In this one Proverb, we see the *Dalet* and the *Gimmel* coming together. There is a blessing that flows from living with an open heart—a symbolic open door—towards people who are in need.

dal	gamal
LAMED – DALET	LAMED – MEM – GIMEL
דל	גמל

DIGGING DEEPER

Read Deuteronomy 15:7–11 and Matthew 10:42. What ministries in your local area help the poor and needy? What could you do today to support those ministries and be an open door?

_____

_____

_____

_____

_____

_____

Extending Kindness

There is a beautiful picture of extending kindness found in the Temple, the house of God located in Jerusalem. In the same place where Yeshua went up to worship, there was a room named the Silent Chamber. People would go into the room and shut the door behind them. The wealthy would enter to deposit money for those in need and then leave. A poor person would come into the room, take what they needed, shut the door, and leave. All of the giving and taking was done secretly. This activity in the Silent Chamber embodied the essence of the *Gimmel* and the *Dalet*—the one who gives and the one who needs takes. *Mishnah Shekalim* states:

"This *mishnah* discusses how people could give charity in secret either to the Temple or to the poor. We should note that in Rabbi Moses Ben Maimon's discussion of charity he states that the second best form in which to give *tzedakah* [charity] is neither for the giver to know the receiver nor for the receiver to know the giver. The only way that was preferred over secrecy was when helping a person earn his own living."[1]

We all should embody generosity towards the poor. Yeshua said in Luke 12:33–34, "Sell your possessions and do *tzedakah* [charity]. Make money pouches for yourselves that do not get old—a treasure in the heavens that never runs out, where no thief approaches and no moth destroys. For where your treasure is, there will your heart be also." In Matthew 5:42 Yeshua reminds us, "Give to the one who asks of you, and do not turn away from the one who wants to borrow from you." Yeshua's teaching emphasized giving to those that have need.

This teaching speaks to each one of us. In the Sermon on the Mount, Yeshua says "Blessed are the poor in spirit, for theirs is the kingdom of heaven (Matt. 5:3). Blessed, or praiseworthy in Hebrew is the word *ashrei*. What does this verse mean? It doesn't mean that we must sell all our possessions and have nothing if we want to be able to enter the Kingdom. A poor person, as we've seen, is one who is dependent upon someone who is wealthier than

....

1 "English Explanation of Mishnah Shekalim 5:6:1," Sefaria, accessed January 22, 2024, https://www.sefaria.org/English_Explanation_of_Mishnah_Shekalim.5.6.1?lang=bi.64.

they are. The poor in spirit is the one who shows complete dependency upon God. They realize that everything that they have comes from Him. Each one of us needs to be like the *Dalet*, recognizing that we are poor and lowly. The door to the kingdom requires us to be, *Dalet*, a poor person, at least poor in spirit. We must understand that God lifts up the poor; He exalts the humble. Being poor in spirit means that we recognize that apart from God, we have nothing. We can't earn our way into heaven and every blessing in our lives comes from Him. He is the one who is the *Gimmel*, the one who bestows beneficent kindness upon us. Apart from Him, we have absolutely nothing. We can't earn our way into the Kingdom.

DIGGING DEEPER

Read Luke 14:12–14 and James 2:5. The great eighteenth-century hymn-writer and ex-slave trader John Newton marveled at the far-reaching implications of these words. "One would almost think that Luke 14:12–14 was not considered part of God's word," he wrote, "nor has any part of Jesus's teaching been more neglected by his own people. I do not think it is unlawful to entertain our friends; but if these words do not teach us that it is in some respects our duty to give a *preference* to the poor, I am at a loss to understand them."[2] In what ways does our

2   John Newton, *The Works of John Newton*, Volume 1 (Carlisle, Pa.: Banner of Truth edition, 1985), p. 136.

own self-focus and even pride get in the way of serving others? What are ways you can show kindness to those less fortunate?

_____

_____

_____

_____

_____

_____

_____

The Posture of Humility

Being like the *Dalet* means to become humble and poor in spirit. Notice the *Dalet* is bent over in a posture of humility to enter the kingdom of heaven. Those who are proud and self-reliant will not enter the Kingdom of Heaven. The letter *Dalet* points to one who lives from a state of sincere and utter dependence upon the Lord.

Psalm 30:1 says, "I will exalt you, ADONAI, for you have lifted me up, and did not let my enemies gloat over me." The Hebrew word for "lifted me up" is *dalah* which begins with the letter *Dalet*. *Dalah* has the connotation of lifting a bucket of water from a well. God intentionally lifts us from the well of our difficulties.

dalah
HE – LAMED – DALET
דלה

Psalm 113:7 says, "He raises the poor from the dust and lifts the needy from the ash heap" (NIV). When the psalmist wrote the word "poor" in this verse, he used the Hebrew word *dal*, which is connected to the letter *Dalet*. The following verse states, "to seat him with princes, with the princes of His people." God is in the business of raising up the lowly, and humble. When we make ourselves lowly and humble, the Lord will lift us up. We read, "Humble yourselves in the site of ADONAI and he shall lift you up" (James 4:10 TLV).

DIGGING DEEPER

Read 1 Samuel 2:7–8, and Psalm 107:41. What is humility? How does pride keep us from the blessings God has for us? In what ways can you begin to develop more humility and less pride in your life?

_____

_____

_____

_____

_____

A Deeper Look at the Number 4

Four is 3 +1. If three represents the Divine as we've taught, the number four is the next step—His creation. The number four refers to all that is created

4 and Creation

- The fourth day saw the material creation completed. The fifth and sixth days involved "furnishings"—animals and people.
- There are four "ancient" elements of creation in the physical world: fire, air, earth, and water.
- There are four states of matter: solid, liquid, gas, and plasma.
- Creation consists of humans, animals, vegetation, and inanimate objects.
- Days are divided into four divisions: morning, noon, evening, and midnight.
- There are four seasons of the year: spring, summer, autumn, and winter.
- There are four directions of the compass: north, south, east, and west.
- The book of Genesis refers to four matriarchs or *imahot* in Hebrew: Sarah, Rebecca, Rachel, and Leah.

- A family can be comprised of a father, mother, son and daughter. This is the fulfillment of the first commandment to be fruitful and multiply and fill the earth.
- There are four letters in the ultimate Divine Name (YHVH). *Yod*, *Hey*, *Vav* and *Hey* is the name God revealed to Moses in the burning bush. It's the name by which God redeemed Israel out of Egypt.

4 and Redemption

At the Seder, the Passover meal, we drink four cups of wine. The four cups correspond to the four expressions of redemption God gave to the children of Israel.

- There are four cups at the Passover Seder in fulfillment of Exodus 6:6-7, "Therefore say to *Bnei-Yisrael*: 'I am ADONAI, and I will bring you out from under the burdens of the Egyptians. I will deliver you from their bondage, and I will redeem you with an out-stretched arm and with great judgments. I will take you to Myself as a people, and I will be your God. You will know that I am ADONAI your God, who brought you out from under the burdens of the Egyptians.'"

The four cups of the Passover are also connected to the four letters of God's name because all the Lord was involved in the redemption of his children from slavery.

- The number four is connected to the gathering of His people from the ends of the world. Isaiah 11:12 tells us, "He [The Lord] will lift up a banner for the nations, and assemble the dispersed of Israel, and gather the scattered of Judah from the four corners of the earth.

- Four is also linked to exile and redemption. There were four stages to the Fall in the Garden of Eden. They were doubt, disbelief, denial, and disobedience which led to expulsion from the Presence of God.

4 and Freedom

Historically, Israel experienced four exiles: Babylonian, Persian, Greek, and Roman. When Yeshua died on the cross, He addressed all four aspects of exile: spiritual, emotional or psychological, relational, and physical. We were disconnected and distanced on all four of those levels. When Yeshua said, "My God, my God, why have you forsaken me (Matt. 27:46 NKJV)?" He's faced the spiritual dimension of exile. When the darkness covered the heavens, Yeshua felt the psychological and emotional pain of disconnection and abandonment from the Father. Yeshua spoke directly to relational exile in at least two instances. First, when He looked at the people and said, "Father, forgive them, for they do not know what they are doing" (Luke 23:34). Then, when Yeshua turned to one of the thieves being crucified with Him and said, "I tell you, today you shall be with Me in Paradise" (Luke 23:43). He was bringing relational reconciliation and forgiveness, reversing that aspect of the Fall while hanging on the cross.

While on the cross Yeshua was wearing a crown of thorns. A crown of thorns is the sign of the physical curse of creation. Genesis 3:18 says, "Thorns and thistles will sprout for you." By wearing the crown of thorns, He was reversing that physical curse and restoring God's original blessing for humanity. There are now four aspects of healing because Yeshua died on Calvary's tree:

- Spiritual healing—you can experience salvation for your soul.
- Emotional inner healing—God can transform the emotional traumas and the dramas in your life.
- Relational healing— He has given us the ministry of reconciliation. God can restore and heal whatever brokenness there is in your relationships.

- Physical healing—Messiah Yeshua is our healer for sicknesses and diseases.

DIGGING DEEPER

We see redemption throughout the Scriptures. Read Psalm 130:7 and Romans 3:21–24. We have been redeemed by Yeshua Messiah. While we all fall short at times, we remain right with God. Still, we often try to be perfect, assuming God is going to be angry with us. How does redemption, our freedom from the four elements of exile, free us from those thoughts?

_____

_____

_____

_____

_____

Dalet and Yeshua's Ancestry

Consider the human ancestry of Yeshua-Jesus. The promised Redeemer would come from what tribe? Judah. The name Judah in Hebrew is *Yehuda*. *Yehuda* יהודה has five letters, four of which are found in the Divine Name (YHWH יהוה). Besides those letters, Yehuda has one additional letter, *Dalet*. It's worth noting that the *Dalet* is inserted between the third and the fourth letters of his name. Why? Messiah is the *Dalet*. The Messiah will come from the family of Judah. He will come from the house of David. David's דוד name is spelled with three letters, *Dalet, Vav, Dalet.* David's name begins with *Dalet* and ends with *Dalet.*

Psalm 145:14 says, "The LORD upholds all who fall and lifts up all who are bowed down" (NIV). The Lord lifts us up. It's a picture of the Son of David, Yeshua, who made Himself lowly and the *Dalet* in David. Yeshua made himself *dal* (lowly). Philippians 2:8 says, "He humbled Himself—becoming obedient to the point of death, even death on a cross." Yeshua made Himself spiritually lowly (*dal*), so that you and I might become spiritually rich. He became lowly so that we might be lifted up. The *Dal* and *Yehuda* represent God redeeming us through the Messiah from the four corners of the earth. He opens the door of redemption for us. Yeshua is the door that brings more. He brings salvation into our lives. He's the door for the poor, for those of us who have nothing that gives us the right to stand before God. You can't earn your way to heaven. You are poor, but through Him you're made rich. That's our Yeshua, the descendant of David from the tribe of Judah.

DIGGING DEEPER

Read Proverbs 15:33 and Hebrews 5:5–7. Yeshua is the door. He stands and knocks, but the doorknob is on our side. We must open it for Him to come into our lives and change them. We must open the door to redemption and His blessings. What keeps people today from opening this door? Why do they fail to see the blessing of becoming rich, while poor?

_____

_____

_____

_____

_____

_____

_____

Dalet and the Shema

The most foundational prayer for Jewish people is, *Yisrael, Adonai eloheinu, Adonai echad.* "Hear O Israel, the Lord our God, the Lord is one" (Deut. 6:4). In the handwritten Torah scroll, the scribe wrote the last letter of the last word (*echad*, "one") with a large *Dalet*. This is true in many Hebrew prayer books as well. Why? When we're praying the *Shema*, we're saying that God is King over all the earth. He's King over the four corners of the earth. We're asking that His redemption spread over the four corners of the earth, and this is fulfilled at the Second Coming of the Messiah. We read of the ultimate fulfillment of this larger *Dalet* in Zechariah 14:9, "ADONAI will then be King over all the earth. In that day ADONAI will be *Echad* [One] and His Name *Echad* [One]."

echad

אֶחָד

When the Messiah comes to establish His kingdom, God's people will be one and have a full realization of His Oneness. And His oneness is the ultimate sign that the Kingdom of God has come on earth, as it is in heaven. May that day come speedily and soon!

DIGGING DEEPER

Read Luke 1:32–33 and Revelation 17:14. Yeshua's reign at His Second coming will be universal. He will be the only God worshipped. In your mind, what does that future look like? How does this future promise of His Kingdom and Oneness affect your daily life?

_____

_____

_____

_____

_____

_____

SUMMARY

Friends, until that day comes, we need to be like the *Dalet*. We need to recognize our dependence upon the

Lord and humble ourselves in His sight. Then, He will lift us up. We need to open our hearts by opening our door to the poor and giving thanks to God for the redemption that He's brought through the son of David. Yeshua is the embodiment of the *Dalet*. He became poor so that you and I could become rich and inherit the kingdom of God. I don't know about you, but I am so grateful for all He's done in my life! I know that I am richly blessed with Him, but apart from Him, I have nothing. May you be blessed and may you humble yourself and experience God's goodness in your life.

What one thing stood out to you in this chapter? Why?

_____

_____

_____

_____

_____

_____

_____

_____

_____

_____

The Letter *Hei* and the Number Five ה

OVERVIEW

The fifth letter of the Hebrew alphabet is the letter, *Hei* (pronounced "hey"). It has the sound of "h" as in "hay." *Hei* has a numerical value of five. Hay is representative of the five fingers of the hand. *Hei* can mean "seed," or "behold", as in beholding the Lord. And it's connected to God's divine breath. Psalm 33:6 says, "By ADONAI's word were the heavens made, and all their host by the breath of His mouth." The Talmud tells us that the phrase "the breath of His mouth" refers to the "sound of the letter *Hei*—the outbreathing of the Spirit."[1]

1   The William Davidson Talmud (Koren – Steinsaltz, Menachot 29b, https://www.sefaria.org/Menachot.29b.2?ven=William_Davidson_Edition_-_English&vhe=Wikisource_Talmud_Bavli&lang=bi

Abraham and Sarah

We see the significance of the letter *Hei* in the story of Abraham and Sarah. When God first appeared to Abraham and Sarah, their names were Abram and Sarai. In Genesis chapter 12, God said to them, "I'm going to make your name great. You're going to become a great nation." Years passed and they had no children. God appeared to them again. Abram must have been wondering if His promise of children and a nation would ever materialize. In Genesis chapter 15, God said to Abram, "Your reward is going to be great." Abram responded, "but I have no children."

God told him to step outside of his tent. He said, "Look at the stars of the sky, if you can number the stars in the heaven, so shall your descendants be." Then something unexpected occurred: God changed their names. Abram became Abraham and Sarai, Sarah. God added the same letter to their names — the letter *Hei*. It was only after God added the letter *Hei* to their names, that they were able to conceive and have a child. In Jewish thought, *Hei* symbolizes the power to be able to conceive.

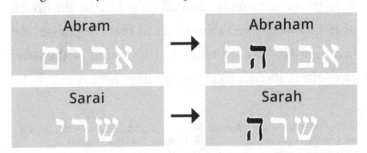

Abram		Abraham
אברם	→	אברהם
Sarai		Sarah
שרי	→	שרה

The letter *Hei* signifies the creative power and potential to birth promise (or children) into reality.

To put this teaching into perspective, we need to look at Genesis 2:4. In Hebrew this passage reads "*elleh toldot hashamayim veha-aretz b'hebaram.*" These five words are "the generations of the heavens and the earth when God created them." What's significant about that the phrase "when God created them" is that it has a letter inserted into the verb *bara* that normally shouldn't be there. It is grammatically incorrect. The letter *Hei* is inserted in the middle of the verb *Bara*. Why? Because *Hei* represents the Divine Breath. Psalm 33:6 says, "By ADONAI's word were the heavens made, and all their host by the breath of His mouth." The breath of His mouth created the hosts of heaven. According to a Jewish understanding, *Hei* is the first sound from which all sound emanated from because *Hei* is the sound of the breath.

Sarah was barren. God added the letter *Hei* to her name, which is symbolic of the letter of creative power, the Divine breath, and the letter of the Divine promises. Sarah was "dead" on the inside. She was a woman in her nineties who should not be able to have children. By adding the letter *Hei*, God divinely breathed new life into Sarah. Just as God breathed the breath of life into Adam, He divinely breathed into Sarah to renew, transform, and empower her to give birth.

Just like God breathed into Sarah, He wants to breathe

into you. He wants to breathe on your promise and your potential. He wants to activate all His power in you and see every promise He's made to you come to pass. You have the potential to "give birth," but you need to experience God's divine breath to make it a reality.

DIGGING DEEPER

Read John 20:19–22. How does Jesus respond to the fear of His disciples? What power did Jesus give His disciples so they could accomplish their mission? What power does God give you? What keeps you from drawing on that divine breath?

_____

_____

_____

_____

_____

_____

Joseph

Hei isn't only connected to Abraham and Sarah. It's also connected to Joseph. Joseph's brothers rejected him. He was in the pits, and then in prison where he interpreted dreams. A couple of years later, Joseph stood before Pharaoh to interpret his dream when no one else could.

Psalm 81:5, says, "He set it up as a testimony in Joseph, when He went throughout the land of Egypt, I heard a language I did not understand." In Psalm 81, the letter *Hei* is added to Joseph's Hebrew name יהוסף (*yeh-ho-safe'*). In Jewish thought, God added the letter *Hei* to Joseph's name because it was the Divine Spirit, the divine breath (symbolized by this letter) that enabled him to interpret dreams. This same divine breath gave Joseph the wisdom and revelation necessary to speak to Pharaoh about the meaning of his dreams and counsel him on what to do for Egypt. Much like God created the world with His breath, He wants to breathe new life into us by His Spirit, symbolized by the letter *Hei*.

DIGGING DEEPER

Read Zechariah 4:6, John 15:5, and Philippians 4:13. How clear is God's message to us about the difference between self-power and His Divine power? How has God's Spirit empowered you during difficult situations?

Divinity and the Divine Name

Hei can also symbolize divinity. Oftentimes in Jewish writings, the letter *Hei* symbolizes the name of God, because the Hebrew word often used for God, *Hashem* means "the name." Many Jewish people don't say God. Many don't say ADONAI. God is often referred to as *Hashem* הַשֵּׁם whose first letter is *Hei*.

The letter *Hei* also symbolizes the Divine Name. In the Divine Name, (YHWH, Jehovah, or LORD in English translations)—*Yud* י, *Hei* ה, *Vav* ו, *Hei* ה—notice that two of those four letters (the second and the fourth) are the letter *Hei*. Most Jewish people don't pronounce the Divine Name when they're not praying. They just say *Hashem*. In Jewish writings, when the name of God is abbreviated, oftentimes, it's written with the letter *Hei* with a Geresh (h'), symbolizing *Hashem*, or YHWH.

You may remember from earlier chapters that the majority (almost all) Hebrew letters are constructed by using other Hebrew letters. The letter *Hei* is constructed with the letter *Dalet* and the letter *Yod*. Why is this meaningful? *Dalet* represents this physical world and the letter *Yod* represents the spiritual world. The rabbis tell us that this world was created with the letter *Hei*. The world to come will be created with the Hebrew letter *Yod*, which we'll look at in a later chapter because *Yod* is the first letter of Yeshua's name.

Why is this combination of letters significant? Part of our calling is to bring the divine breath into the physical world. We elevate the material world by making God's Spirit the center of everything we do. As we learned, *Dalet* stands for brokenness and *Yod* symbolizes God's extended hand to bring God into the situation. In so doing, we sanctify the physical and bring spirituality to it.

DIGGING DEEPER

Read Psalm 34:17–20. When is the time we are most likely to ask, "where is the Lord?" This Psalm says that's when He is the nearest. How affirming is it to you that when you're in tights spots, the Lord is there extending His hand? What is your response?

_____

_____

_____

_____

_____

The Upper Room

In John 20:22, we read, "He breathed on them. And He said to them, 'Receive the Ruach ha-Kodesh!'" The sound that symbolizes Yeshua breathing on them is _Hei_. That moment echoed the Creator breathing into the first humans and Abraham and Sarah receiving new names (featuring _Hei_). Yeshua filled the disciples with the Holy Spirit because they were beginning the first mission, which is ultimately fulfilled in the Great Commission to be a blessing to all nations.

DIGGING DEEPER

Read Genesis 2:7 and Psalm 33:6. At the first post-Resurrection meeting with the disciples, Jesus breathed

His Spirit on them (John 20:22). Why did He say He was doing this? We recognize that God speaks to each believer by His Holy Spirit. What assurance does that give you as you read about Abraham, Joseph, and the disciples?

_____

_____

_____

_____

_____

_____

Divine Revelation

We also notice a link between the letter *Hei* and divine revelation. God breathed into the soul of man. 2 Timothy 3:16 says, "All scripture is God breathed." This "Spirit origin" of the biblical text explains why our engagements with Scripture bring such life and empowerment to our souls. Think about it on this level too: the Word of God is the breath of God. It's divinely breathed (*theopneustos* in Greek). *Hei*, the breath of God, has the numeric value of five.

- How many books are there in the Torah? There are five (*Hei*) books.
- God gave Moses two tablets at Mount Sinai. On each of those tablets there were five (*Hei*)

commandments. The five commandments on the first tablet relate to loving God, the five commandments on the second tablet relate to loving your neighbor.

In the Ten Commandments, we discover the number five (*Hei*) in connection to loving God and loving our neighbor. Obviously, we broke those Ten Commandments. However, when Yeshua died on the cross, he died at the intersection of those "two fives"—the vertical and horizontal commandments to love the Lord your God and love your neighbor as yourself.

In the ancient Hebrew pictograph form, the letter *Hei* looks like someone raising their hands. This makes sense because when we behold God, experience salvation, and encounter His Word, what else can we do but lift our hands and praise His name? *Hei* is not just tied to Scripture and divine revelation, but to salvation itself. The reason being that one of the primary biblical words for salvation begins with the letter hei. Hoshia as we read in Psalm 118:25 "Lord save us" (Lord save/ hoshiah us).

ה - HEI

Behold, reveal, breath

DIGGING DEEPER

Read Mark 12:28–34. We've talked about the Shema which is what Yeshua quotes here. Why is it important to love God? How will loving God help you to love others?

_____

_____

_____

_____

_____

_____

Divine Redemption

Remember, David killed Goliath with five smooth stones. Why did he pick up five smooth stones? For one, it represents divine creative power and the potential to overcome the forces of chaos. Goliath represented chaos, like "in the beginning" when the Spirit of God hovered over the waters. Like God added the *Hei* to Abraham, Sarah, and Joseph's names, empowering them to walk in His purpose and power, David needed the *Hei*/five stones (symbolic of the Divine Spirit) to be victorious!

Hei and the number five also have a place at the Seder, the Passover table. In our last chapter we spoke of the four Passover cups based on God's four "I will" statements. But there's a fifth which is, "I will bring you into the land of Israel, the promised land" (Exodus 6:8). *Hei* is associated with this fifth cup, the cup of Elijah.

Elijah prepared the way of the Lord, as the Prophet Malachi wrote: "Behold, I am going to send you Elijah the prophet, before the coming of the great and terrible day of ADONAI" (Malachi 3:23). Five is symbolic of the ultimate redemption that the Messiah will bring. He's going to raise us above "the four." He's going to bring us into "the five" when He gathers us from the four corners of the earth and brings us into the promised land of Israel. Elijah's (fifth) cup points to this.

DIGGING DEEPER
Read Isaiah 26:3 and John 14:27. The world is full of chaos. How do you cope with it? How did David or Joseph cope with the chaos in their lives?

_____

_____

_____

_____

_____

Divine Repentance
The letter *Hei*, symbolizes repentance, in Hebrew *teshuvah*. The letter *Hei*, has a small opening on the left side. What does the small opening represent? Even when we turn from God, He always leaves the door cracked open for us to

return to Him. We can see this in an interesting way in the Passover. The word *matzah* מַצָּה, unleavened bread, is the symbol of the great redemption and the word *hametz* חָמֵץ is the Hebrew word for leaven. During Passover, you must remove all the *Hametz* because it's the picture of sin and slavery. These two words share the same letters, except for one. The word *hametz* has the letter *Chet*, and *matzah* has the letter, *Hei*. The letters are nearly the same shape, but the letter *Chet* used in *Hametz* (leaven) is connected or closed. There's no opening. *Hei* represents repentance because it has a crack, meaning we can always return from *hametz* (leaven sin). With no opening in *Hametz*, there's no return.

There's no salvation without repentance. As the Apostle Peter proclaimed, "Repent, therefore, and return—so your sins might be blotted out, so times of relief might come from the presence of ADONAI and He might send *Yeshua*, the Messiah appointed for you" (Acts 3:19-20). This concept is something that's missing today in the Gospel message. We call people to receive Yeshua so they can experience life, blessing, and heaven. But friends, you can't turn **to** God without turning **from** sin. We must leave the leaven behind and turn towards Yeshua and His salvation, which is represented by the *matzah*. The other interesting thing is that there are several letters in the Hebrew texts that have little crowns on them (when written by a scribe).

The letter *Hei* is one of them. Why? Because it symbolizes when we return to Him and repent, He crowns us. There's a crown waiting in heaven for all those who repent and become sons and daughters of the king.

DIGGING DEEPER

Read Isaiah 62:3 and 1 Peter 5:4. Is your focus more eternal or temporal? Did you know you have a crown awaiting you? How does your life change because you have a crown waiting for you in heaven?

_____

_____

_____

_____

_____

SUMMARY

Hei reminds us that we are royalty and God wants to breathe new life into us. He wants to breathe into our promise and potential. This includes you too! He wants to bring out the fullness of everything that He's promised to you. He doesn't want you to live a barren life. It doesn't matter how old or young you are. Like Abraham and Sarah, when you allow Him to breathe into you, new possibilities can be birthed, no matter what your circumstance is! If you return to the Lord and constantly seek

Him, you'll discover an open door (*Hei*) of opportunity. He will crown you and you will see Him do great things for you. May we soon see the day when the *Hei* is fulfilled and Messiah returns, bringing us all to the New Jerusalem to worship Him forever!

What part of this lesson was most valuable to you? Why?

_____

_____

_____

_____

_____

_____

_____

_____

_____

_____

VAV

ו

6

The Letter *Vav* and the Number Six ו

OVERVIEW

The Hebrew letter *Vav* is the sixth letter of the Hebrew alphabet and has a numeric value of six. *Vav* is pronounced in modern Hebrew as a "v" sound (as in "vine") and has a similar shape to a hook. *Vav* in Hebrew means "hook." A hook is something that links and connects to things. *Vav* or hooks connected the columns in the Tabernacle (Exodus 26:32, 37; 27:10).

A Connecting Conjunction

In Hebrew, the letter *Vav* is used as the conjunction "and." Whenever you say or write "and" in Hebrew, you insert *Vav* as a prefix in front of the word. A conjunction

connects two things, including two sentences, or two words. Thus, the letter *Vav* is all about connection. We find this from the beginning of the Bible. Genesis 1:1, says "In the beginning, God created the heavens and the earth." God created the world in six days, and He rested on the seventh. It's noteworthy that Genesis 1 has seven words corresponding to the seven days of creation. The sixth word of Genesis 1:1 begins with the letter *Vav*. "In the beginning, God created the heavens and *[Vav]* the Earth." *Vav* is what connects heaven and earth.

> "AND" (AS IN, "AND THE EARTH") IS VE'ET
>
> **ואת**
>
> IN HEBREW

Vav and Six
Six and the Physical

The letter *Vav* represents the number six, which symbolizes the physical realm. Consider the dual aspects of the three dimensions: length that has front and back, breadth that has right and left, and height that has up and down. All physical space or objects connect to the six dimensions. In this way, the number six (*Vav*) represents something that is surrounded on all sides. In Scripture we read that God surrounded Israel in the wilderness (Ex. 13:21)—front, back, left, right, up, and down. That's part of the reason why on the Feast of Tabernacles (or *Sukkot*), we shake the *Lulav* and the *etrog*[1] in all six directions.

What's also interesting in Hebrew, the word for the number six is *shesh*, and when we add its letters, they total 600. Why is that important? Because the Greek word

SHESH (6)

$$ש + ש = 600$$

kosmos (world) also equals 600. The phrase "God made" in Greek also equals 600. Let's look at Acts 17:24, "The God who made [*poieó* / 600] the world [*kosmos* / 600] and all things in it, since He is Lord of heaven and earth, does not live in temples made by hands." This passage is an example of how in both biblical languages *Vav* and six point to the physical world. "Six" is connected to "600" which, in turn, links to the world and God, the One who made heaven and earth.

DIGGING DEEPER

Read Psalm 139:7 and James 4:10. When Israel journeyed through the wilderness God's presence surrounded them. All six sides were covered. God protected and provided for the children of Israel. Do you feel God's presence in

1 The *lulav* and *etrog* are just two of four types ("species") of plants that worshipers hold and wave during *Sukkot* (Leviticus 23:40). The *lulav* is a palm branch (combined with myrtle and willow branches) and an *etrog* is a citron fruit.

your life? Share a time when you've felt surrounded on all six sides by your loving, heavenly Father.

_____

_____

_____

_____

_____

_____

Six and Redemption

Six is also significant in terms of redemption. Six is the number of man because God created man on the sixth day. But something else occurred on the sixth day—the Fall. According to Jewish Tradition, humanity lost six things as a result of man's sin: radiance, life, height, the produce of the earth, the fruit of the tree, and the luminaries of Divine Light that shone upon us in the Garden of Eden. Remember, the shape of *Vav* is like a hook, and therefore a symbol of a connector. The *Vav* is a reminder of the connection and His redemption.

Genesis 2:4 reveals something amazing to us: "These are the generations of the heaven and of the earth when they were created, in the day that the LORD God made earth and heaven" (JPS).

The word "generations" is important in the book of Genesis and throughout the Bible. The phrase "these are the generations" forms the outline of the book of Genesis. The Hebrew word for "generations" is *toledot* תּוֹלְדֹת. In Genesis 2:4, *toledot* is written in its complete form with two letter *Vavs* in it. Yet in every appearance of *toledot* throughout the Hebrew Bible after Genesis Chapter 2 (except for one), it is missing one of the *Vavs*. Why? Because, when we sinned, we broke the connection between heaven and earth. Ever since, those six things we mentioned earlier have been missing. So, the mystery of the missing *Vav* points to the fact that we fell on the sixth day and lost connection to those six things.

toledot in complete form	*toledot* in defective form
תּוֹלְדוֹת	תּוֹלְדֹת

There's only one place in the Old Testament where *toledot* is not written defectively. Ruth 4:18–22, that begins, "These are the generations [*toledot*] of Perez." This verse speaks to the genealogy of King David through Ruth and Boaz, and David's ultimate heir, the Messiah. Why is *toledot* written in full form in the Book of Ruth, Chapter 4? Because it's through David that the Messiah, the son of David, will come—the one who will redeem humanity from its slavery to sin and restore all things. Six is not only relevant to creation, but its restoration through Yeshua's redemptive work.

Yeshua's first miracle was turning the water into wine

with **six** stone pots (John 2:6). This first miracle gives us a glimpse of the restoration He came to bring, restoring the fruitfulness in the original blessing of creation.

Yeshua died on a tree (i.e., a Roman cross), on Good Friday. Friday is the **sixth** day of the week—the same day man and woman sinned with the Tree of Knowledge. He came to reverse the curse and to restore the blessing. He died on the sixth day to restore the connection between heaven and earth. Yeshua came so we could live the connected life with Him.

DIGGING DEEPER

Read John 10:27–28. Notice Yeshua connected sheep with God's saving hand, which connects to what the Lord did at the Passover by means of a lamb. God revealed His mighty hand at the first Passover and the Last Supper (a Seder meal!). God is all about connection and redemption. How has God redeemed you? How has a connection with Him changed your life?

_____

_____

_____

_____

_____

_____

Six and Revelation

On the sixth day of the month of *Sivan,* God gave the Ten Commandments on *Shavuot* (Pentecost). This day, also referred to as Pentecost, is the same day the Holy Spirit filled the Twelve Apostles (Acts 2). Why is this significant? Because six is three times two, a double portion of the Divine life (represented by the number three). Every commandment in the Torah begins with the letter *Vav.* In the Torah, there are fifty-three portions or readings[2]. All except ten portions begin with a *Vav.*

There are 248 columns in a handwritten Torah scroll. Every column begins with the letter *Vav* except six (the letter *Vav*'s numerical value). *Vav* is the most used letter in the five books of Moses. There are 778 Vavs in the Torah separating the two verses from Genesis 46:8 – Exodus 1:1.

Interestingly, there are sixty-six books in most Christian Bibles because the Bible is meant to bring us into a deeper connection with God and with Messiah, Yeshua.

Six, Cain, and the Commandments

The **sixth** commandment of the Ten Commandments is "You shall not murder." Why is this commandment's placement significant? When Cain killed Abel, God put a mark on Cain to spare his life (from vengeance or

2   For more information about these 53 readings and how you can receive a free Torah Portion Guide, please go to our website, fusionglobal.org.

retribution) out of His grace (*cf.* Gen. 4:15). Jewish tradition tells us that the mark God put on Cain was the letter *Vav.* Why the *Vav*? Because when God asked Cain, "where's your brother," Cain responded, "Am I my brother's keeper?" Cain refused any sense of connection to or responsibility for Abel. He was asking God, "What does he have to do with me? Why are you asking me?" Cain was trying to hide what he did from the Lord. The Lord put the letter of connection as a sign upon his head to remind Cain and everyone who looked upon him that we're all connected. We *are* our brother's keeper. Rabbi Larry Raphael, senior rabbi of Congregation Sherith Israel in San Francisco put it this way:

> *For this [act of murder], God sentenced him to permanent exile. And God put a mark upon his forehead. And what was that mark? It was the letter vav. You will be sentenced to wear the letter vav on your forehead for the rest of your days so that you and all those who see you will realize and know that you are connected to others. You are your brother's keeper. And so is every other human being.*[3]

3 Rabbi Larry Raphael, "The Lessons of the vav: We're defined by our Connections to Others, March 13, 2010, https://www.jweekly.com/2010/03/13/the-lesson-of-the-vav-were-defined-by-our-connections-to-others/

Six and the Cities of Refuge

There are six cities of refuge (Num. 35:6–15)[4]. The primary purpose of these cities was to protect a person who had accidentally killed (Num. 35:6f; Deut. 19:2f) someone (often called manslaughter or justifiable homicide in our legal system). The person would be safe from the avenger—a family member charged with avenging the victim's death (Num. 35:19). However, *Talmud Mikkot* reminds us that murderers who intentionally killed someone were there as well.[5] The six cities of refuge were in different areas of the Land of Israel so everyone had reasonable access to them. The southernmost city was Hebron; the northernmost was Kedesh, in the Galilee; and the city of Shechem was in the center. At roughly the same latitudes, three more cities were chosen on the other side of the Jordan River.

In the cities of refuge, we see God's hand of redemption at work. The accused's life was not put at risk by arbitrary actions of the avenger. An impartial court would decide the question. If the person was found innocent and vindicated, he or she spent the rest of their lives in the city of refuge. Much like believers who become conscious of sin through actions they could have avoided,

....

4 To the west of the Jordan: Kadesh, Shechem, and Hebron. To the east of the Jordan: Bezer, Ramoth, Golan.

5 English from The William Davidson digital edition of the Koren Noé Talmud, with commentary by Rabbi Adin Even-Israel Steinsaltz, 10a7–12, https://www.sefaria.org/Makkot

we flee to a refuge in Messiah. We are forgiven and we continue to live in His refuge.

Six and the Mark of the Beast

The number six connects to 666, the mark of the beast (Revelation 13:18). As we stated, six is the number of man and the physical world. Now let's also consider that whenever something is repeated three times in Scripture, it means the maximum, much like adding multiple exclamation points. 666, then is the number six expressed to the highest degree. It represents "earthiness" or materialism at the highest level. The mark of the beast points to the inordinate emphasis on the physical or material realities.

Satan's goal is for humanity to focus on our physical needs at the expense of our souls, leaving us no better than animals. Hence, rather than God's image, we would bear the mark of the beast (666) in the world. Keep in mind that what separates us from the beasts is the image of God and the breath of life in us, as we saw with the letter, *Hei*.

DIGGING DEEPER

We've looked at several aspects of the number six—the physical world, redemption, revelation, the Ten Commandments, cities of refuge, and the Mark of the Beast. How will you read or look at the number six differently in the future? Which aspect of six stood out most to you? Why?

Generations

But of course, there is still even more concerning the letter *Vav*. As we mentioned earlier in this chapter, the Hebrew word for generations is *toledot*. We said that after the Fall, in the Hebrew Bible, one of the *Vavs* is missing from the word *toledot*. We also noted how the word generations (*toledot*) is significant in the book of Genesis. But here's what's interesting. There are three primary genealogies in the book of Genesis: the genealogy of chosen people (through Isaac), the genealogy of the descendants of Ishmael, and the genealogy of the descendants of Esau. Each of these genealogies is written slightly different concerning the *Vav*. Let me explain.

When the Bible lists the genealogies of Abraham and his descendants, they include the first letter, *Vav*, but the word is always missing the second *Vav*. The first letter *Vav* reminds us of the covenant and of the Torah that God gave on Mount Sinai on the sixth day. Remembering this event reconnects us to relationship and understanding of the Lord. The letter *Vav* is written in the genealogies of the Jewish people like Abraham and Isaac because they and their descendants were ultimately going to receive the Torah. Still, their genealogies are missing the second letter, *Vav*. Why? Because the second *Vav* reminds us of Yeshua, the Messiah, who died on the sixth day. He restored the *Vav* (connection) that was broken. He gave the Holy Spirit on Pentecost (Acts 2). Jewish people are pointing to a secret, a mystery. Jewish people have the Torah and the Hebrew Scriptures. Still, apart from a remnant of people like me, they have not received the Messiah yet. One day, however, they will receive Him, restoring the second *Vav*. It's for their redemption that we pray and labor.

Then there's Ishmael's genealogy (Gen. 25:12–16). When *toledot* is written, it doesn't have any *Vavs*. It's written doubly defective, missing both *Vavs* because Ishmael's posterity never accepted the Torah. The word misses the first *Vav* because the Ishmaelites don't rightly honor the Bible—they read the Quran. They are also missing the second *Vav* because they also don't have the New Testament. They don't believe in Yeshua in a biblical way, and they don't have the Holy Spirit. So, Ishmael, who represents Islam, is missing both *Vavs* because they don't have the Torah or the New Covenant, and they don't have Yeshua as their ultimate Savior and Redeemer.

Now, let's examine Esau. When the Bible gives us his generations, it misses the first *Vav*, but has the second

Vav. What does this teach us? In Jewish tradition, Esau represents Christianity and believers in Yeshua. This is a fantastic thought connected to the letter *Vav*. Why? Esau's genealogy misses the first *Vav* because Christians, for the most part, have historically forsaken the Jewish roots of their faith. They lack a Jewish understanding of the Scriptures. Still, Esau's genealogy has the second *Vav*, because Christians embrace New Covenant.

In Matthew 13:52, Jesus says, "Therefore every Torah scholar discipled for the kingdom of heaven is like the master of a household who brings out of his treasure both new things and old." Friends, don't settle for half an inheritance. We need the "Old and the New" for a complete connection. You can't only have the Old because the Torah is not enough to save. But at the same time, you need the New. If you have the New without the Old, you're still missing something. It would be best if you had the **roots** (Old Testament) and the **shoots** (New Testament) to bring forth the maximum amount of **fruit** in your life. It will help if you put down roots that make shoots that lead to leaves of belief and helping others.

The Torah was ultimately intended to point to the Messiah, who is the fullness and fulfillment of it all. The second *Vav* which Christians have is the New Testament and the Holy Spirit. It's sufficient for salvation, but it's not the full inheritance. Ultimately, Jew and Gentile, old and new, need to come together for the fullness of God's promises and blessings to be released into the world. Pastor Jon Courson tells us,

> *"If we get stuck in the old and are not open to what the Lord is doing presently, we'll miss what the Lord is doing creatively in this day. But if we're only into the new and fail to draw from our history and heritage, we'll become spiritual lightweights and airheads. Jesus said the one who receives from both old and new will be a rich man."*[6]

What about you? Are you stuck in the New or the Old? What benefits do you find when you connect both Testaments?

The letter *Vav* connects with *teshuvah* (repentance). Why? Because when you turn the *Vav* on its side, it's the letter of the shofar—a musical instrument made from a ram's horn often used in military settings (Lev 25:9; Josh 6:4–20). Outside of warfare, the horn was used in ritual settings. It announced *Rosh Hashanah* and the coronation of kings.[7]

....

6 Jon Courson, *Jon Courson's Application Commentary* (Nashville, TN: Thomas Nelson, 2003), 98.

7 John D. Barry et al., eds., "Shofar," in *The Lexham Bible Dictionary* (Bellingham, WA: Lexham Press, 2016).

The sound of the shofar calls us to return to God and the fullness of the teaching and impact of His Word in our lives. Most importantly, the sound of the shofar points to the coming of Messiah who will restore the fullness of the connection between heaven and earth.

The full connection comes when you have both *Vavs*. That is what our ministry, Fusion Global, is all about—restoring the *Vavs*, connecting you to the roots of your faith in Yeshua. When you have the *Vav* in your life, you're connected. I encourage you to continue to study and discover how the old and the new are connected. As a result, your life will overflow with blessing, much like those six stone pots in John 2. You won't live out of the lack, but out of the overflow on every level.

1 Corinthians 15:51–54 says:

Behold, I tell you a mystery: We shall not all sleep, but we shall all be changed—in a moment, in the twinkling of an eye, at the last shofar. For the shofar will sound, and the dead will be raised incorruptible, and we will be changed. For this corruptible must put on incorruptibility, and this mortal must put on immortality. But when this corruptible will have put on incorruptibility and this mortal will have put on immortality, then shall come to pass the saying that is written: "Death is swallowed up in victory."

Friends, this final scene is related to what Paul discussed in Romans 11. When Messiah comes at the sound of the shofar, the world will see Him. The eyes of the Jewish people will be opened, as will the eyes of the nations. Salvation will come. The connection will be restored, leading to the Kingdom and complete restoration.

SUMMARY

Connection and redemption are the fulfillment of the letter *Vav* and the number six. The *Vav* reminds us of the connection between the Old and the New. The number six is deeply symbolic of physicality and repentance.

What did you find in this chapter that meant the most to you? Why?

_____

_____

_____

_____

_____

_____

_____

_____

_____

_____

_____

_____

ZAYIN

ז

7

The Letter *Zayin* and the Number Seven ז

OVERVIEW

This chapter examines the letter *Zayin*, the seventh letter of the Hebrew alphabet. It is pronounced "ZAH-yeen" and has the sound of "z" as in zebra. *Zayin*'s numerical value is seven. It also means "weapons." Additionally, *Zayin* means *zun*, "to sustain."

Seven is a tremendously significant number in the Bible. As we've talked about in other chapters, the names and shapes of the Hebrew letters are meaningful. The name *Zayin* means "crown." *Zayin* also means "sustenance, or to sustain." The Hebrew root word for sustenance or provision is *zun*. *Zayin* is also connected to the Hebrew word for sword (or weapons). The top of the *Zayin* is the handle, and the vertical leg is the blade.

The *Zayin*'s shape is an upside-down sword, much like a sword that's been stuck in the ground. The sword in the ground is prophetically relevant to the Messiah, as we're going to see by the end of this chapter.

Zayin, Seven and Creation

As I've mentioned before, Genesis 1:1 has seven words in it: *Beresheet bara elohim et hashamayim ve'et ha'aretz.* Why seven words? Because Genesis 1:1 is a summary of the seven days of creation. Since God completed the heavens and the earth in seven days, the number seven symbolizes completion. We must note that God rested on the seventh day. The seventh day is associated with the *Shabbat*, the Sabbath, the most important day of the week. It's a day to examine the world around you and understand that everything (His completeness) comes from God. On this day we cultivate our trust God as our Provider. By observing the seventh day as Sabbath, God provides the *Zayin* (the sword or weapons) to overcome negativity and the attacks of the devil.

The Menorah

The seven words of Genesis Chapter 1 also connect to the seven branches of the Menorah, the golden candelabra that stood in the Holy Place in the Tabernacle and the

Temple. Today, the Menorah is the seal for the modern-day State of Israel. The menorah's seven branches correspond to the seven days of creation. The three branches  on the one side of the Menorah point to the first three days of creation; those on the other side, to days four through six. The middle branch symbolizes the Sabbath, because all its wicks face it. Everything points to the Sabbath (*Shabbat* in Hebrew). Yeshua Messiah is the ultimate fulfillment of the Sabbath. He will usher in the Messianic Age, the time that is **all** *Shabbat*. In the Menorah we see that all the days of the week (and by extension, all time) point to the ultimate Sabbath—the Messianic Kingdom—which is our return to the Garden of Eden.

Zayin, Seven, and Revelation

Zayin and the number seven not only point us to the first week of Creation and the New Creation in the Messianic Kingdom, but to revelation. Remember when we taught about the letter *Vav* and the number six? God came down on Pentecost (*Shavuot*) on the sixth day of the month of Sivan. However, God gave the Torah on the Sabbath, the **seventh** day of the week. The foundation of the Scriptures—the first five books of Moses and God's Covenant with Israel—is linked to the number seven. But there's more . . . The Hebrew word for "seven" is *Sheva* שֶׁבַע.

You write "7" with the Hebrew letter *Zayin*, but when you speak Hebrew, "7" is *sheva*. *Sheva* has a lexical connection to the word meaning "to swear or an oath." That's a critical detail because God's Word is His promise to us. Everything that God has promised is located in His Word. It's as though God took an oath. Every promise in His Word will come to pass. Seven is also the number of covenant. The promises in God's Word are covenantal in nature. God never revokes His covenant. He never cancels His promises. The Bible is the Almighty's Word of promise and a source of supernatural hope for you and me.

DIGGING DEEPER

Read Luke 24:27. Jesus was talking to His disciples after His resurrection. They were slow to understand, and Yeshua made it clear that all the Bible points to Him as the ultimate fulfillment of the Sabbath. In what ways does knowing this teaching help you to better read and understand your Bible?

Provision

When we study God's Word, He moves us towards completeness in Him. Now let's consider the connection between not only seven and creation and revelation, but its connection to God's sustenance and provision. One of God's promises is that we will prosper if we meditate upon His Word day and night. Psalm 1:2–3 tells us, "But his delight is in the Torah of *ADONAI*, and on His Torah, he meditates day and night. He will be like a planted tree over streams of water, producing its fruit during its season. Its leaf never droops—but in all he does, he succeeds." As I've mentioned, God is known to many Jewish people as *Hashem* (meaning "The Name"). He is the unchanging God who is faithful to us. He's our Sustainer and Provider. *Zayin* is connected to the root word for sustenance, the nourisher.

DIGGING DEEPER

Read Joshua 21:45 and 1 Kings 8:56. How does knowing that God keeps His promises give you confidence in your day-to-day life?

_____

_____

_____

_____

_____

_____

Zebulun and Issachar

Zayin also connects to the tribe of Zebulun, one of the twelve tribes of Israel. The name Zebulun זבולון begins with the letter *Zayin*. The tribe of Zebulun descended from Jacob's third youngest son (Leah's youngest son). Zebulun's territory was located on a ridge between the Jezreel Valley and the Turan Valley, between the territories of Naphtali and Issachar.

The tribe of Zebulun entered a partnership with the tribe of Issachar whose border they shared. The tribe of Zebulun were merchants. They were the first international businessmen of the Holy Land. They were in the export business. They came to Issachar and said, "Listen, we're going to do business, and we want to make a deal. You study the Torah and become spiritual scholars and leaders, and experts in God's Word. We will support you in your spiritual endeavors. We will give you a portion of our wealth to underwrite your learning. Then, we want to share your learning and all the spiritual impact, including a reward in the kingdom of heaven." What was the result of such a deal? Both Zebulun and Issachar prospered. 1 Chronicles 12:33 underscores the benefits of this agreement. It says, "from the sons of Issachar—men who know how to interpret the signs of the times to determine what Israel should do." Some of the most outstanding scholars in ancient Israel came from Zebulun because of the Zebulun-Issachar partnership between the marketplace and the ministry. We still need this kind of collaboration and partnership today. It's critical. In his final blessing of the twelve tribes, Jacob blessed Zebulun and Issachar together. The interesting thing is, he should have blessed Issachar *before* Zebulun because Issachar was older. Jacob blessed Zebulun—the younger before the older—because, in Jewish thought, the one who causes something is greater than the one who receives the benefit. Issachar's success in their study of the Torah and their spiritual activities was because Zebulun took care of took care of them, so Jacob blessed them first.

Even today it's not uncommon for successful business people in the Jewish community to go to rabbis, scholars, or organizations and financially support them with this principle in mind. This is a wonderful thing. God's people need to partner with those who are teaching and speaking the Word. "The worker is worthy of his wages" (1 Tim. 5:18). Those who seek a reward in heaven and abundant life should consider these sorts of strategic Kingdom partnerships.

DIGGING DEEPER
Read Genesis 49:13 and Deuteronomy 33:18–19. What benefits do you see in partnering with a ministry that is teaching and expounding God's Word?

‎_____

‎_____

‎_____

‎_____

A Connection to Manna

God provided manna (Ex. 16:31) from heaven for six days of the week as a "bread from heaven" (Ex. 16:4; Psa. 78:24). Manna was the Children of Israel's primary source of food until they settled in the Promised Land, where they would eat the "produce of the land" (Ex. 16:35; Josh. 5:12). On the sixth day, He provided a double portion (Ex. 16:5) of manna that sustained them on the seventh day, the Shabbat. As a result, the people didn't have to work or gather on the seventh day. The provision of manna taught the Children of Israel not to be afraid but to trust God and have faith in Him as their Provider. They had to trust God daily for their portion and not hold it overnight—there was only enough for the day (Ex. 16:4, 16–19). Then, on the sixth day, they had to trust God the opposite way— that the manna wouldn't putrefy and would last for two days when they collected the double portion.

Yeshua referenced the daily manna collection when, in the prayer He gave the disciples, He said, "Give us this day our daily bread" (Luke 11:13 KJV). There is so much spiritual insight connected to manna. For example, what changed for the Children of Israel when they came into

the Promised Land and the manna from heaven stopped?
Two things. God declared that every seventh year was the
Shmita, the sabbatical year. The Torah calls for the Jewish
people to work the land for six years and rest the seventh (Lev. 25:1–8). They were to let the land lie fallow.
There are two lessons within this point. In addition to
replenishing the land, God was trying to make sure they
never forgot the lesson of the *manna*, even in the Promised Land. Just as the Children of Israel had to trust God
in the wilderness for the seventh day, they would have
to trust God's provision during that seventh year in the
Promised Land. The *Shmita* gave the land rest, but this
downtime also gave the people an opportunity to focus
more intensely on spiritual matters.

Secondly, people typically say a blessing *before* the
meal. But, Deuteronomy 8:10 says, "So you will eat and
be full, and you will bless ADONAI your God for the good
land He has given you." In the Torah, the blessing is first
commanded after eating meals. Why? Forgetfulness. God
warned Israel that when they entered the Promised Land
and ate from a vineyard they didn't plant and grew fat
that they were vulnerable to forget the Lord. They might
presume their blessings were the result of their efforts,
instead of God's faithfulness. This blessing after meals is
known as *Birkat Hamazon*. The word *hamazon* comes
from the word *zun*, which means sustenance, and begins
with the letter *Zayin*.

It reminds us that God is our provider. *Ochel*, the Hebrew word for "food," has the numerical value of 57 (note it has a "7" in it). Dagan, "grain" also has a numerical value of 57. *Osher*, "wealth" in Hebrew has a numerical value of 570 (any number multiplied by ten signifies completion or perfection). Wealth is the perfection of God's sustenance (food and provision). There is a link between the concepts of completion and perfection to the *shmita* (or "sabbatical") year—the double portion of *manna* on the Sabbath. This connection extends to the Year of Jubilee (Lev. 25:8) that happened after seven sabbatical annual cycles—every 50th year. Just like the sabbatical year, Jubilee was a time of freedom. It reminds us that freedom comes from trusting the Lord to provide. If you're living in fear and anxiety, you have no freedom. God invites us to walk and work in the freedom and rest that flows from our faith and trust in Him as our Provider.

DIGGING DEEPER
Read Nehemiah 9:15–16 and Philippians 4:13–19. When have you seen God provide supernaturally for you? How did it feel to know how much God cares for you to live in peace, faith, and rest?

_____

_____

_____

_____

Strength and Provision

One word for "strength" in Hebrew is *oz* עֹז and it has
a numerical value of 77. God gives the strength needed
to earn our sustenance. We don't overcome challenges by
our own strength, but as we trust the Lord to fight our
battles, much like Israel at the Battle of Jericho. Hence,
the number seven is also connected to warfare. *Zayin* is
in the shape of a weapon. Remember what happened at
Jericho (Josh. 6). They marched around the city one time
for 6 days and on the seventh day they marched seven
times. Then, at the sound of shofar blast and Israel's battle cry, the wall came tumbling down! One reason the
Israelites circled the city seven times is the association of
"7" with warfare and weapons. *Zayin* is also associated
with overcoming, a phenomenon that also happens to
relate to God's provision. Think about it: the Children of
Israel overcame their enemy, not by their own hands, but
through God's provision of a rather unique battle plan.

We find God's provision in the New Testament and
a specific connection to Yeshua. In Matthew 14, the disciples are with Yeshua and a large gathering of 5,000 men
(plus women and children!). Yeshua told the Twelve to
feed the multitude but they didn't know how they were

going to do it. They looked among the crowd, and all they could find were five loaves and two fish. Why that number? It totals a number seven. Seven is the numerical value of the Hebrew word for "fish," which is *dag*. They used fish and bread. The word *Sheva* ("seven") in Hebrew has the same root as the word for "satisfaction." Yeshua took the five loaves and the two fish, and He multiplied them. He is the Provider. He is the One who is the source of sustenance for all of us, and for the world. He used the fish, which equals the number seven because he's trying to communicate that there's always more than enough. And with Him, there's always the promise that we will leave more than satisfied (there were leftovers on that day).

DIGGING DEEPER

Read Joshua 1:9 and Psalm 46:1–3. God is a God who gives us strength when we need it and provides for our needs. How have you seen God's strength manifested in your life? How has His strength helped you through troubled times?

_____

_____

_____

_____

_____

_____

Seven and the End Times

Seven also has a connection to End Times. We read in Revelation 15:1, "Then I saw another great and wonderful sign in heaven: seven angels who have seven plagues—the last ones, for with them God's wrath is finished [complete]." It further says they overcame the Beast and his image, and they sang the Song of Moses and the Song of the Lamb. As the Book of Revelation unfolds, we read about seven angels' seven plagues, the seven bowls, and then everything is finished within seven years. As we mentioned earlier, seven is the number of warfare. In the End Times, God will wage spiritual war, and bring history to a conclusion, to completion.

Seven is the number of completion and perfection. Seven is also the number of satisfaction. Seventy times seven equals 490. 490 is a numerical value of the Hebrew word *tamim*. It means "to be perfect or complete." Being

tamim (490)

תמים

FINAL MEM + YOD + MEM + TAV = 490
70 X 7 = 490

perfect or complete connects to God's promises and His covenant, symbolized by the seven colors of the rainbow in the days of Noah. The rainbow is the sign of God's promise that He will not destroy the earth by a flood again. The Bible is full of His promises. We need to know and declare them! This (at the time of publication) is the "Decade of the *Peh*" (the 5780s on the biblical calendar), the decade of breakthrough and the mouth (*peh* is "mouth"). Let's declare His promises with our *peh*!

SUMMARY

- *Zayin* means a crown, and it points to the Messiah who wears the crown. He is the one who brings the world to completion and perfection. He is the one who ushers in the Messianic Age associated with the number seven, a time that is all Sabbath that brings rest, peace, and Shalom to the world.
- *Zayin* is the sword pointing upside down. Why is that important? Because Messiah is the one that will bring shalom peace between nations as it says in Isaiah 2:4, "they will beat their swords into plowshares."
- *Zayin* is connected to God's Word. It reminds us of God's promise. Psalm 146:10 says, "ADONAI will reign forever, your God, O Zion, from generation to generation. Halleluyah!" The connection being made here is that Zion begins with the hebrew letter Zayin. When will you reign in Zion, Lord? May it be speedily and soon.

- *Zayin* means provision. May you trust God for your provision. May you not strive but remember the seven to rest in Him. He is your sustainer. He is your provider. Just as Yeshua multiplied the bread and the fish, He can multiply the meager resources you have in your hand. If you are willing to partner with Him (like Zebulun and Issachar), investing in His Kingdom, and crown Yeshua as king over your life, He will give you strength to overcome your enemies. I hope you experience that power of the *Zayin* in your life and have faith to believe what He will do for you.

What was most important to you in this chapter? Why?

_____

_____

_____

_____

_____

_____

_____

_____

_____

CHET
ח
8

The Letter *Chet* and the Number Eight ח

OVERVIEW

This chapter looks at the eighth letter of the Hebrew alphabet: *Chet* (rhymes with "met" or "mate"). When pronounced, *Chet* has the sound of "ch" as in "Bach." Being the eighth letter of the Hebrew alphabet, *Chet* has the numerical value of eight. *Chet* symbolizes *chai*, which is the Hebrew word for "life." We see this symbolism in the actual shape of the letter, which resembles a bride and groom standing under the wedding canopy. As we know, the shape of every Hebrew letter is created using other letters. So, the letter *Chet* is comprised of the letter *Vav*, which symbolizes the groom, and the letter *Zayin*, which symbolizes the bride. At the top, there's a little point that connects them (in its traditional, scribal format), representing the wedding canopy, which in Hebrew is *chuppa*. The pictorial imagery in the Hebrew letters is so rich!

TWO LETTERS COMBINE TO CREATE *CHET*

ZAYIN – VAV

CHET

The wedding theme is evident not only in the shape of the letters coming together, but also in the numerical value of those two letters. As we've already learned, the letter *Zayin* equals seven, and the letter *Vav* equals six; seven plus six is thirteen. Why is that significant? Because thirteen is the numerical value of the Hebrew word for love, *ahava*. It's also the numerical value of the Hebrew

word *echad*, which means "one" as in, "Hear O Israel, the Lord our God, the Lord is **one**"—*echad*. Notice that the letter *Chet* is right in the middle of the word *echad*. Love unifies us in one true fellowship (John 17:22–23). Genesis 2:24 talks about husband and wife becoming one flesh—*Basar echad*.

Life, Love, and Creation

All these themes come together in the structure of the *Chet*: life, the bride and groom, the wedding canopy—love. Thirteen (*Zayin* plus *Vav*) is the number of love and the number of oneness. 1 Corinthians Chapter 13 is the "love chapter" in the Bible (and it has thirteen verses). Therefore, it makes sense that *Chet* is the letter of life because **life comes through love**—both spiritually with the Lord and physically between people, between the bride and the groom.

Life and love connect to creation. The first woman's name was Eve, *Chavah* חוה in Hebrew. *Chava* links to the word *chai*, which means "life." The name "Eve" begins with the letter *Chet*. And "Eve" is linked to life because she is the mother of life. Life and love are connected to the original commandment, which was to be fruitful and multiply and fill the earth (Gen. 1:28). The marriage between Adam and Eve embodied this commandment, as they brought forth life in the world. These profound realities are all connected to the name, the symbolism, the number, and the meaning of the letter *Chet*.

DIGGING DEEPER

Read Genesis 9:1 and Psalm 127:3–5. Describe the connection between the first commandment in Genesis 1:28 and life and love.

_____

_____

_____

_____

_____

The Redeemed Life

Chet has meaningful connections, not only to creation, but also to redemption. How is this? Consider how the Hebrew Scriptures describe the process of making atonement. The priesthood and the Tabernacle were an integral part of this critical reality, which foretold the redemption that would ultimately come through the Messiah.

When the Lord told Moses to dedicate the Tabernacle (Num. 7:1), Israel was to take it up and down for seven consecutive days. On the eighth day, the Levites were to erect the Tabernacle (long-term) amid the people until God told Moses to break it down and take it away. On the eighth day they erected the Tabernacle, and officially inaugurated it by offering sacrifices. On the eighth day, then, God's Presence entered the Tabernacle. The high priest wore eight vestments (see Exodus 28). Eight spices were used to make the Tabernacle's anointing oil and incense. Eight poles were used to carry the holy vessels—two each for the Ark, the Table of Showbread, the Golden Altar, and the Copper Altar. The Levites used eight instruments to make music before the Lord: seven plus their voices.

There were eight sprinklings of blood by the high priests on *Yom Kippur*, the Day of Atonement. There were eight sprinklings because eight is connected to life and redemption. "For the life of the creature is in the blood, and I have given it to you on the altar to make atonement for your lives—for it is the blood that makes atonement because of the life" (Lev 17:11). *Yeshua* spilled His blood to make atonement for us for our salvation. The functions of the priesthood on *Yom Kippur* foreshadowed our redemption and the Lord's provision for our salvation.

DIGGING DEEPER

Read Leviticus 23:36. Redemption and atonement (or at-one-ment) are critical terms for us to understand. How do you define redemption? How is life connected to it?

_____

_____

_____

_____

_____

_____

The Grace Connection

Eight is also the letter of grace. The Hebrew word for
"grace" is *chen* חֵן, which begins with the letter *Chet*.
This letter's association with the grace of God is crucial
because salvation is *by grace*. There's a fantastic example
of the link between *Chet* and grace in the Hebrew Scriptures. Psalm 145 is one of the primary psalms that Jewish
people read three times a day. This psalm is an acros-
tic, meaning each verse is connected to a letter of the alphabet. The eighth verse is tied to *Chet* and contains the
phrase *channun ve-rachum:* "gracious and compassion-
ate is the Lord, slow to anger and abounding in kindness."
Grace is kindness given from God that we don't deserve.
There is nothing we can do to earn it; it is a free gift from
Him. Grace is also divine assistance and empowerment
that fills-in what is lacking in our lives. We need the *Chet*,
and we need the *chen*, the **grace** in our life that brings
divine empowerment.

Genesis 6:8 says, "Noah found grace [*chen*] in the
eyes of the Lord" (NKJV). There are links between Noah

and grace and the number eight. Grace enabled him to build the ark against all odds and sustain himself during all the laughing and jeering against him. He and his family experienced salvation, which is by grace. "For by grace you have been saved through faith, and that not of yourselves; it is the gift of God" (Eph 2:8 NKJV).

DIGGING DEEPER

Read Exodus 34:6–7 and Ephesians 2:8–9. How would you define the glory of God? How would you define the grace of God towards you? What words would you use to help a friend understand glory?

_____

_____

_____

_____

_____

Yeshua's Supernatural Life – Living from the Eight

As we've mentioned, eight is connected to creation. It's connected to redemption, priesthood, and atonement. It points to salvation by virtue of its relationship to the concept of grace. But of course, there's even more—the number eight points us to Yeshua's life, death, and resurrection. How? The Messiah died on a Friday, which is the sixth day of the week on the Hebrew calendar. He was in the grave part of that sixth day and all the seventh day, the Sabbath. Just as God completed the work of creation in six days and then rested on the seventh, so Yeshua finished the work of redemption and rested on the seventh day. Of course, He then rose from the dead on Sunday. We all think of Sunday as the first day of the week. In one sense it obviously is, but from another perspective, Sunday is also the eighth day. If Friday is the sixth day and Saturday the seventh, then Sunday is the eighth day. This detail matters because in Jewish and biblical thought, eight is the number of the supernatural—one step above the natural order (seven). More specifically, we need to understand that eight is the number of resurrection.

In Greek, *Yeshua's* name adds up to 888. He's the "Son of David" who was the eighth son of Jesse. Yeshua is the one who transcends death. He's the one who breaks through the boundary of the grave. And since we are "in Him," we rise as He was raised. Supernaturally, the same Spirit that raised Yeshua from the dead lives and dwells in us (see Rom 8:11). When we "live from the eight," we live from the supernatural state.

Considering these insights, God's command that Abraham institute circumcision on the eighth day is much more meaningful. Jewish people have circumcision (*brit milah*) on the eighth day, because eight is symbolic of covenant as well as the supernatural. God was putting a supernatural mark in the flesh of the Jewish people. Why? So that we can never be destroyed. The Jewish people have a covenant in their bodies that's connected to the supernatural. We mentioned that seven is the number of "completion" of this world. There are seven days in a week. God gave Noah the rainbow with seven colors. There are seven Noahide Laws—seven universal commandments given to all humans. But $8 = 7 + 1$—a supernatural state—it goes beyond the natural order of this world.

The premise is that circumcision on the eighth day raises the Jewish people above this physical and material reality, leading to a supernatural existence. This connection to "eight" explains the Jewish people's "supernatural" survival through centuries of persecution and Israel's rebirth as a nation-state. The Jewish people are "eighth-day people." And through Yeshua the Messiah, believers are circumcised from the heart, raised with Him, and seated with Him in heavenly places. We are an "eighth-day" people! We can rise above every situation and circumstance supernaturally in Him.

In addition, eight is the number of new beginnings. We see this in circumcision as well—on the eighth day, it's a new beginning for a Jewish baby boy. According to Peter's epistle (1 Pet. 3:20), eight people walked out of Noah's ark after the Great Flood (*mabul hagadol*) and stepped into a new beginning. The Lord reaffirmed His covenant with Abraham eight times. Sukkot is an eight-day festival that anticipates the World to Come. Even in music, there are seven notes on the diatonic scale and the eighth begins anew on a higher level. These phenomena point to the resurrection and new beginnings.

Eight is the number of transcendence, of rising above. As we said, seven represents the completion of the natural world. God created the heavens and the earth in seven days. Eight symbolizes breakthrough, going beyond the natural order of things. Eight signifies the ability to overcome, to rise above barriers and the confines of the material world. It's the life of overflow.

DIGGING DEEPER

Read Colossians 3:12–14. Rabbi Paul lists seven "graces" or keys for God's people. In verse fourteen we discover a critical eighth key. What is it? How does it unite the others? How does this lone, over-arching key give you a breakthrough life?

The Yoke of Discipleship

Finally, the number eight is profoundly meaningful on a practical level because it represents a call to discipleship. The design of the letter *Chet* also resembles a yoke. A yoke connects two animals together, typically for use in farming. There are three yokes for us to consider.

- There is a literal yoke, used to connect animals so that they could pull a plow, moving and working together in partnership to get the work done.
- There is a yoke related to God's Kingdom. In Jewish thought, when we say the words of the *Shema*— "Hear O Israel, the Lord our God, the Lord is One. Blessed be the name of His glorious kingdom forever and ever"— we're taking upon ourselves the yoke of the kingdom of heaven. Each one of us need to take upon ourselves the yoke of the kingdom of heaven and be committed to His rule and reign under His guidance.
- There is also a third yoke, the yoke of discipleship. When a disciple formally followed a rabbi, he was committed to taking on the "yoke" of the rabbi—taking on the teaching of the rabbi, living according to everything

that he learned from his master. This is what Yeshua meant when He said, "Take My yoke upon you and learn from Me, for I am gentle and humble in heart, and 'you will find rest for your souls.' For My yoke is easy and My burden is light" (Matt 11:29-30). Friends, discipleship is being yoked to Yeshua as He leads and teaches us.

The rabbis called their students to acquire three things. First, there is the call to acquire a spouse, to be yoked to a life-partner. Hence, the Apostle Paul's admonition, "Do not be unequally yoked" (see 2 Cor 6:14). Don't marry someone who isn't a believer, who doesn't have the faith. Second, there's the call to connect to a rabbi. Everyone needs a rabbi. We need to be yoked to a teacher because our need to learn never ends. More than encouragement, we need the transformation that comes from the renewing of our minds (see Rom 12:2).

And then thirdly, there is the call to find yourself a friend. In Hebrew, this is the word *chaver*. This friend is not "one of the guys" to watch sports with or someone to go "hang out with your girls." It's a spiritual friend, someone to study and grow with as "iron sharpens iron" (Prov 27:17). We need these three levels of relationship of being yoked. We need to have those people who join us on our journey of faith. When we are connected on these three levels, we fully experience the growth and discipleship that the Lord wants for us.

DIGGING DEEPER

The critical question is: will you take the yoke? Will you take the yoke of the Kingdom on yourself? Will you take the yoke of learning from a rabbi and studying with others (as iron sharpens iron)? Because when you take the yoke, it leads to life (*chai*) and God's blessing. Life is born out of relationship and community. If you want to be fruitful and multiply and fill the world with God's blessing and salvation, then you need to do it in partnership with others.

What hinders you from taking the yoke and breaking through to new relationships, new study of God's Word, and a life born out of relationship?

_____

_____

_____

_____

_____

_____

_____

_____

_____

_____

SUMMARY

We've studied the letter *Chet* and number eight in this chapter. We discovered:

- Love and life connect to creation.
- Eight connects to redemption, the priest-hood, and the Tabernacle—all of which foretold the redemption that ultimately came through Yeshua Messiah.
- *Chet* and *chen* (the Hebrew word for grace) point to salvation by grace.
- Yeshua's supernatural life and breakthrough are available to all of us as we "live from the eight."
- The potential and power of the yoke of discipleship.

Which of these topics from our study of *Chet* meant the most to you? Why?

_____

_____

_____

_____

_____

_____

_____

About the Author

Rabbi Jason Sobel grew up in a Jewish home in New Jersey. In his late teens, Jason set out on a quest to discover the truth. After years of study, he discovered and embraced his true destiny as a Jewish follower of Jesus. As the founder of Fusion Global, Jason's purpose is to bring people's understanding of Jesus into high-definition by revealing the lost connection to our Hebrew roots and restoring our forgotten inheritance in Him.

Rabbi Jason received his Rabbinic messianic ordination in 2005 and has a BA in Jewish Studies and an MA in Intercultural Studies. He is the spiritual advisor to *The Chosen* TV series and host of several TBN programs. He is the author of several books—including national bestsellers *Mysteries of the Messiah* and *The God of the Way*—and a much-anticipated new release in the fall of 2025. Rabbi Jason also leads and organizes rabbinic study tours to Israel and Greece at rockroadrabbitours.com. Find him on YouTube and Instagram at @RabbiJasonSobel and rabbijasonsobel.com

Aleph

(silent, "ah-lef")

Faces Right »

1

Oneness | Chief | Strength | Ruler

 GET THE VIDEO COURSE

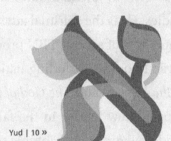

« Yud | 10

Yud | 10 »   « Vav | 6

Ancient   Middle   Late
Pictogaph   Hebrew   Hebrew

GET MORE IN THE
TEACHING LIBRARY

Fusion Foundations
Seven Sessions
Course
★★★★★

Letters and Numbers
Volume 1,
Aleph - Chet
★★★★★

Best of Rabbi Jason Sobel
Stand-Alone
Sermons
★★★★★

Mysteries of the Messiah
TV Series
Twelve Episodes
★★★★★

Aligning with God's
Appointed Times
Livestreams, Teachings, and Specials
★★★★★

The Birth of a Jewish King
Six Sessions
The Christmas Story Revealed
★★★★★

Mysteries of the Messiah
Podcast
Teachings, Show Notes, Special Guests
★★★★★

Walking with Rabbi Jesus
Eight Episodes
The Resurrection of the Jewish Messiah
★★★★★

Torah Portion Guides
and Teachings
Past PDF's Included
★★★★★

EXPERIENCE THE LAND OF THE BIBLE
IN HIGH DEFINITION

Experience The Bible With
Rabbi Jason Sobel

Ready To Book A Life-Changing Experience?

ROCKROADRABBITOURS.COM

You're invited

TRIBES! *with Rabbi Jason Sobel*

GOD IS GATHERING TRIBES TO EXPERIENCE THE BIBLE IN HIGH DEFINITION - TOGETHER

A **Fusion Tribe** is a small, local Bible study group that meets regularly for discipleship and community, utilizing **Fusion Global** resources to guide each gathering.

FUSION TRIBES
WITH RABBI JASON

FUSIONGLOBAL.ORG/TRIBES

IF YOU'RE SEEING THIS, YOU'RE ONE OF US!

Made in the USA
Monee, IL
11 March 2025

13605243R00085